Momin Movement
and
Ansari Community

Golden Chapter from India's Freedom Struggle

Momin Movement and Ansari Community

[A Saga of Struggle and Sacrifice during India's Freedom Movement]

Khurshid Anwar Arfi

SHIPRA

Rs. 650; US$ 32.50

ISBN: 978-81-7541-840-0

First Published in India in 2016

Momin Movement and Ansari Community

Published by:
SHIPRA PUBLICATIONS
LG 18-19, Pankaj Central Market, I.P. Ext.
Patparganj, Delhi-110092, India
Tel: 91-11-2223 5152, 2223 6152
E-mail: info@shiprapublication.com
www.shiprapublication.com

Begin with the Name of All'ah
The Most Benevolent and Merciful
Lord of All the Worlds
All Praise for Him
His Manifestation of Mercy and Magnanimity
Bestowed upon me the Honour
To Pen the History of this Great Nationalist Movement

Dedicated to
The fond memory of
My most loving
And respectful parents
Whose affection and guidance
Inspired me to struggle
To scale Height of honour
And popularity

Foreword

It is my pleasure to pen the foreword of the new book of Khurshid Anwar Arfi on a very important historical subject related to the national freedom movement.

Momin movement played a very significant role during India's struggle for freedom spearheaded by the Indian National Congress. The Momin community stood firmly against the communal politics of Muslim League and rejected the demand of a separate homeland for Muslims.

Arfi had been closely involved with the activities of the Momin movement for the last five decades. He was a close associate of the legendary Momin leader, Abdul Qaiyum Ansari. This itself ensures the authenticity of this historical book.

For its distinct role during freedom struggle, Momin movement occupies a place of honour and dignity in the pages of history. This publication of Arfi also carries his research work on the subject of Arab ancestry, a branch of Ansaris, which creates interest in the minds of the readers.

I am confident; this will be yet another precious addition to the writings on India's freedom movement.

This book should be a source of inspiration for younger generation.

Dr. A.R. Kidwai
Former Governor, Bihar, Bengal & Haryana
Ex-Member, Rajya Sabha
Ex-Chairman, UPSC

Contents

Words from Author

Since long I had the spirited desire to pen the history of Momin movement which scripted a golden chapter of the contemporary Indian history.

It is a unique and most inspiring story of a depressed section of the Muslim community who was being humiliated and subjugated for centuries and how they could gather strength and conviction to fight against the social evils that had plagued the life of the Indian Muslims and struggle against the mighty British Empire. It is a story of unshakable determination, strong sense of patriotism and sacrifice. The movement with its unflinching faith in secularism and communal harmony must for a strong and united India, left deep impression on the hearts and minds of every Indian and has found a place of honour in the Indian history.

When I first unfolded my idea to pen the history of the Momin movement to those with whom I had been quite closely associated for long, personalities like Dr. A.R. Kidwai, former Governor, B.R. Bhagat, also a former Governor and Lok Sabha speaker and late Budhdeo Singh, former Bihar minister and a close friend of mine, welcomed the idea as they were unanimous in their opinion that a person like me who was all along and still deeply involved in the present day activities of the historical movement should write his personal account and experiences in the shape of a book which will go down as a valuable contribution to the Indian history. However, it was Dr. Kidwai's continuous pressure that came as a great inspiration for me to write this book.

My Interest in the Movement

Being in the depth of the Momin movement since last six decades, my interest with this movement dates back to my childhood days when I came into contact with Abdul Qaiyum Ansari, who later became the legendary figure of the movement and a top Congress leader, being quite close to my father and used to visit our place very often in Gardanibagh colony of government quarters in Patna. I, vividly remember that it was one Sidheshwari Prasad Sinha of Dehri-on-Sone, a noble soul, who, since day one, almost on all occasions used to accompany him. In later years, I could make out that their friendship was exemplary that continued life long. Even during the peak days of his engagements both as a minister and a senior congressman of the state, A.Q. Ansari used to visit Sidheshwari Babu's residence at Boring Canal road every evening consistently. All I could gather that during their meetings besides family affairs was that they usually discussed Indian National Congress and the Momin movement. However, the seeds of the movement were sown in the early 20th century and took formal shape as early in 1924 itself. With the passage of time, both my curiosity and interest in Congress and Momin movement grew.

Abdul Qaiyum Ansari could sense my inclination towards the Momin movement. Occasionally, he used to take me with him in its meetings where I could get interest in its deliberations and speeches of the elders. My interest further grew during the election campaign for 1946 assembly elections held on the basis of separate electorate. I remember the election scenario. A couple of Muslim parties mainly Muslim League and Momin Conference were in the poll fray. The main rival was Muslim League. The Election Commission was not there and campaign was a fun during those days. There were separate boxes for voting. Momin Conference had red and Muslim League, green. Red flags in our hands, our slogan was *'Momin Conference Ko vote Do, Lal Buks Mein vote Do'* (Vote for Momin Conference, put your vote in red box).

First Congress government was formed with Dr. Sri Krishna Sinha as the Chief Minister. Two Momin Conference nominees were taken into the cabinet. Abdul Qaiyum Ansari who had won his assembly seat from Ranchi on Momin Conference ticket, was made a cabinet minister with P.W.D. and Relief and Rehabilitation departments and Abul Ahad Mohammad Noor of Purnia, who had won from Madhubani assembly constituency, became Parliamentary Secretary.

In the year 1948, A.Q. Ansari, who, till now, was the State

President of Momin Conference, was elected President at the national level in place of Sheikh Zahiruddin, Advocate of Ambala who had since resigned and left for Pakistan. Sheikh Zahiruddin successfully piloted the movement during its tumultous period before independence. National session of the Momin Conference was held at sprawling Bankipore Lawn, now Gandhi Maidan, at Patna. It was a festive occasion for the Momin-Ansar community that infused further interest and a good opportunity for me to meet the founding leaders of the movement.

In December 1949, I appeared at Matric exams of Patna University. Around the same period, I lost my elder sister, so shocking to me. Before result could come out, my father, for a change, arranged for my tour to Delhi, Agra and Gandhi Nagar, (now the capital of Gujarat) where first Plenary Session of the Indian National Congress was held. It was a very big area of desert land where the present capital was then proposed. A.Q. Ansari visited Gandhi Nagar with a big contingent of Bihar Momin-Congress leaders including Md. Yasin Ansari, M.L.A., Hazaribagh; Abdur Razzaque Ansari, Irba, Ranchi; Master Abdur Razzaque Ansari, Nalanda; Md. Yasin Ansari, M.L.A., Santhal Pargana; and others.

Gandhi Nagar was then a city of tents and no concrete building was there. The president of Indian National Congress was Patta Bhi Sita Ramaiya. Ansari was very happy to see me there and said—'*Ab Tum Pucca Congressi Ho Gayai*' (Now you are a full fledged Congressman). He purchased a few Congress souvenirs for me which I adorned on my shirt and then, we all went for coffee in a nearby make-shift restaurant. I do not remember every programme but it is still fresh in my mind that when the team went to have an audience with the Congress president, I was also there.

With this sequence of events coming up fast, I found myself in the midst of leaders of both Momin Conference and the Congress party. Sovereign India was the historical achievement of Congress party and that of the unprecedented role of great success played by the Momin Conference. Both Congress men and the Momin-Ansar community were in upbeat mood. Momin Conference had reasons to be doubly proud as their political stand was fully vindicated and had scored over the separatist ideology of Muslim League. With these favourable events, my interest in the movement and Congress party constantly grew.

First Publication

Momin-Ansar community had little knowledge about the details of the Momin movement since its inception till I brought about a special number on the life and achievements of Abdul Qaiyum Ansari, the icon of Momin movement, of my weekly paper '*Sada-e-Hind*' in July 1966. A couple of articles from Maulana Md. Yahya, Barrister Mohiuddin, Hafiz Shamshuddin and other notable persons, all founders of the movement, were highly informative that gave sufficient insight into the movement to its readers besides Ansari's life sketch. At one point of time during early days of my long journalistic career, I wrote an exhaustive article on Momin Movement covering almost full page of Patna's premier English daily, '*Searchlight*' (now its publication has seized) that was widely read all over which gave details of the movement, was highly appreciated by the intellectual class. Sometimes later, All India Momin Conference brought out a booklet 'A Peep into Momin Movement' written by me in English in a precise form. From that period onwards, my special number on A.Q. Ansari and the booklet became the basis for almost all researchers and authors of books that came out subsequently on the life of al:A.Q. Ansari or about Momin movement. However, the first book on the life of A.Q. Ansari in Urdu was published by Bihar Urdu Academy and written by Shahid Ramnagri. It was amazing to find that the book was rather a reprint of 'Ansari number', of special issue of '*Sada-e-Hind*' except foreword inserted by some other person. The author of this book was also an Urdu journalist, and a good friend of mine but he did not show the basic courtesy to mention this fact as a reference in the book which is obligatory for the authors to do so. All the articles on Ansari Saheb were reproduced as such, even without any formal editing. This fact has also been mentioned by Professor Dr. Alauddin Ansari who has subsequently authored his book, 'A.Q. Ansari—Social Philosophy and Political Thought'. He wrote—"It is desirably worth mentioning that Khurshid Anwar Arfi brought out a special number on the life and personality of Mr. A.Q. Ansari on his 62nd birth anniversary in July 1966 under his editorship of Sada-e-Hind, an Urdu weekly of Patna. It was perhaps first collection of articles written by various persons.... Next to Mr. Arfi, Mr. Shahid Ramnagri of Ramnagar (U.P.) compiled a book in Urdu on Ansari Sahib entitled '*Abdul Qaiyum*

Ansari-Hayat Aur Karname' (Abdul Qaiyum Ansari: Life & Works). As a matter of fact it was not a new book. Since maximum articles of the aforesaid 'Sada-e-Hind' edited by Mr. Khurshid Anwar Arfi were recollected."

Another book on Ansari Saheb that too in Urdu was authored by Prof. Mujtaba Ansari. He also took advantage of the articles on Ansari and Momin movement from my publication but was honest enough to give their due references. When I brought out special number of my weekly paper 'Sada-e-Hind' on Ansari Saheb's life and achievements and the small booklet on the movement, I never imagined that the materials provided by me will be a part of history of Momin movement and it was going to be so popular in the community since this proved to be the first source of complete information about such a pioneer movement of the country. Subsequently, I realised that I had done a bit of service in that direction.

In Urdu language, a number of books and booklets were published on Momin Movement from time to time, but none in English language. A related book in Urdu *'Momin Ansari Beradri Ki Tahzeebi Tareekh'* written by Dr. Momin Mohiuddin of Bhiwandi, Maharashtra carries references of a number of publications that dealt on the subject and also of distinguished writers. He has dealt in length mainly on the cultural history of the Momin community of India but it could not provide social and political contributions of the Momin Conference and through it, that of the Momin-Ansar community of India. Scholar in Persian, Dr. Momin Mohiuddin taught the language in the Maharashtra University from where he retired in 1989. He got President's award too for his contribution to Persian literature. Another book in Urdu, *'Momin Conference Ki Dastavezi Tareekh'* written by Ashfaque Hussain Ansari, ex-M.P. and son of the distinguished Momin leader of Gorakhpur, Istefa Hussain Ansari took full advantage of my journal's special number on Ansari Saheb. It is regrettable indeed that Ashfaque Hussain Ansari, out of his undue craze of courtesy, allowed a novice writer and an undesirable person to pen highly objectionable matter against a distinguished personality of the Momin movement. This has definitely robbed the publication of its authenticity. These shortcomings could only deprive the publication of its authenticity. It was for these reasons that the book could not find favour with the readers.

There are several books written by historians, both in Hindi and English, who have made rich references of Momin Movement but confined to its role in the national freedom movement. Perhaps, this will be the first book exclusively on the Momin movement from the days of its very foundation to a full fledged movement along with the most important subject of the origin of the Momin-Ansar community in any language so far. I have earnestly tried to keep this publication completely free from any biased reference to any caste or community, so that no one feels embarrassed or hurt, except mentioning the basic facts about the Momin-Ansar caste or community alone.

Ancestry of Ansaris

Besides Momin movement, I have endeavoured to touch the issue of the origin of a branch of Momin-Ansar community, earlier considered a disgraced caste among the Muslims only in the Indian subcontinent. In India, the purity of Islam was influenced by the religion and culture of the majority community, the Hindus. While the basic tenets of Islam, meaning thereby five time prayers, offering of Zakat, Fasting, Haj Pilgrimage continued in their original form and shape, Hinduism made its greatest impact on the social life of Indian Muslims which continues till today. Not only that, it made inroads into certain religious obligations of the Indian Muslims. The worst to mention is the evil of caste system prevalent in the majority community, where it has got religious sanction too, has made a serious impact on the Muslim society. Like Hindus, Muslims were also divided into upper and lower castes, an evil practice alien to Islam.

On this particular issue, before proceeding, I would make it clear that the theory about the origin of the Momin community in India as suggested in 'Tareekh Momin Ansar' of Maulana Abdus Salam Mubarakpuri's 'Alminwal-w-Ahla' which says that "The entire Momin community of India are the descendants of Oas and Khazraj tribes, ancestors of Hazrat Ayub Ansari." (Reproduced on page 94 of Dr. Momin Mohiuddin's book, 'Momin Biradri Ki Tahzeebi Tareekh') is not acceptable. In my considered opinion, this contention is mere exaggeration and does not conform to facts available; moreover the theory does not go down the throat, as well. I have very cautiously gone through the facts available in the history on this subject and I have taken every care that the present work of mine, like in the past, should strictly be authentic and free from any sort of exaggeration. While it is true that a branch of the Momin-Ansar community in India were the generations of Khazraj tribe to which Hazrat Ayub Ansari belonged, but it is equally true that another large section of the Momin-Ansaris are also convert from Hindus like any other Muslim of this country. The facts on this subject produced by me in this book are based on authenticated historical research.

History and Origin (Wikipedia)

On this subject the comments given by Wikipedia, the online cyclopedia, under title "History and Origin" are however reproduced as such in part, with which I am not obliged to agree in toto. The facts given here are misleading and gives a wrong impession about this noble caste or community.____Author.

"The Momin Ansari, historically known as Ansar or Ansari are a community of Muslim weavers. They (Momin or Ansari) originated in Saudi Arabia. They belong to Hazrat Abu Ayub al-Ansari (Companion of Prophet Muhammad). It is believed that Ansari helped the Prophet Muhammad in escaping from the non-muslim ground, which were coming to kill him.

The community are found throughout East and North India, but Varanasi District, in Uttar Pradesh, is always looked at by most Momin as the centre of their community. In that city, the Ansari are said to make a third of the city's population. Important Ansari neighbourhoods in the city include Madanpura, Adampura and Jaitpura. The Momin of North India are mainly a landless community, but some of them are small and medium scale farmers, and have always been connected with the art of weaving. Some members of the community have entered private or government service. Their relationship with the Sadh community is of some importance, as they supply the Momins with the cotton cloth, used for printing. The Momin do not have any traditional social councils, but have an India-wide community organization, the All India Momin Conference. They are an endogamous community, only rarely marrying out of their group. There is no system of gotras, and cross and parallel cousin marriages are common. The community considers itself to be of Shaikh status, and if no suitable match is found within the group, marriages are acceptable within other communities in the Shaikh category. The Momin are Muslims of the Sunni sect, and are fairly orthodox, but are divided along sectarian lines between the Barelwis and Deobandis. Historically, the community produced the sage and philosopher, Kabir, and some members of the community had been Kabirpanthi. The Ansari are an Urdu speaking community, although the Garana Ansari of Gujarat have Gujarati as their mother tongue.

Bihar: The Ansari community is found throughout Bihar and Jharkhand. In Bihar, they are found in all the districts. They are active in politics. Their socio-economic condition has been improving constantly. They are playing active roles in all walks of life in Bihar. In Jharkhand, they are mainly found in Koderma, Hazaribagh, Gumla, Ranchi, Lohardaga and Singhbhum districts. They speak the Sadri dialect, which is distinctive to the community, although most have the knowledge of Urdu. The community is endogamous, and marry within a close kin group. Like other Ansaris, they were historically weavers, although most of them are medium and small scale farmers. Many of them are market gardeners, and grow and sell potatoes, cabbages and other vegetables, and sell them in Calcutta (now Kolkata) and Patna. The Momin Conference was founded in Bihar, and the Bihar Ansaris have played a key role in the organization.

Gujarat: There are two distinct communities that are commonly known as Momin, the native Gujarati-speaking Garana Ansari, and the immigrant Shaikh Ansari community, originally from North India. The Garana Ansari community in Gujarat are found mainly in the districts of Junagarh, Ahmedabad, Surat and Kutch. They are also known as Turia and Tari. The Momin have eight clans, the Dhoralia, Mehetar, Mithwani, Rajbani, Kora, Chutani, Arbani and Dhorijiwala. They speak Gujarati with substantial Urdu loanwords. In addition to membership of the Momin Conference, the Gujarat Ansaris also have their own caste association, Garana Sayed Fari Jamaat. The traditional occupation of the Ansari is still weaving. Many of them are engaged in zari work, which involves sari embroidery. This is especially the case in the towns of Jamnagar and Dhoraji, which each have traditional quarters inhabited by the Ansaris. Most Surat and Ahmadabad Ansari are now employed in the Bharat Sanchar Nigam Limited clerk posts, and local textile mills.

The Shaikh Ansari are an Urdu-speaking community, and are said to have immigrated from Delhi, Rajasthan and Uttar Pradesh some three hundred years ago. In Baroda, they were invited by the ruling dynasty to help in the construction of public buildings.

The Shaikh Ansari are divided into four endogamous groups: the Bijnor Ansari, originating from the city of Bijnor in Uttar Pradesh; the Ganga Parvala, originating from the village of Gomtipur and its surroundings in Uttar Pradesh; the Delhiwala, originally from Delhi; and finally, the Pratapgarh Ansari originating from the city of Pratapgarh and surrounding areas in eastern Uttar Pradesh. They are mainly distributed in the cities of Ahmedabad, Surat, Bharuch, Baroda, and Rajpipla. Weaving was the traditional occupation of the Ansari, and at present, those in Ahmadabad are still engaged in this activity. Many Ahmadabad Ansari are now power loom owners. But many Shaikh Ansari have also diversified, and now own hotels and bakeries. They are among the most successful Muslim community in the state, having made the transition from their traditional occupation to becoming the successful businessmen. The level of literacy is steadily increasing, and many Ansari are now graduates. The Ansari have no traditional caste association, but are members of the All India Momin Conference. Historically, each of the four sub-divisions would have had their own informal caste association, headed by a chaudhary. These have all but disappeared.

Rajasthan: The Ansari of Rajasthan claim that they were once warriors, who after a defeat in the past, took to the occupation of weaving. They also known as Deswali Shaikh, and speak the Madri dialect, which is a mixture of Urdu and Hindi. They are one of the larger Muslim communities in Rajasthan, and are found in the districts of Tonk, Jaipur and Sawai Madhopur. The Ansari are strictly endogamous and practice both parallel and cross cousin marriages. Their main occupation is weaving, and they use both hand held and power looms. Quite a few are now involved in tailoring and the manufacture of bidis, a local cigarette. The Rajasthan Ansari are members of the Momin Conference, as well as having local informal caste councils, which deal with inter community disputes, while the Momin Conference acts as a pressure group dealing with the state government. The Ansari are Sunni and Deobandi, and have provided many of the Ulema in Rajasthan.

Maharashtra: The Momin of Maharashtra are immigrants from North India. They are split into two groupings, the giyara gaonwala and the bais goanwala, the former are found in Ahmadnagar, while the latter are found near Pune. The Momin were historically a community of weavers, found mainly in the towns and cities of western Maharashtra. They are found mainly in the districts of Pune, Nasik, Ahmednagar, Aurangabad, Jaina, Osmanabad, Dhule, Nagpur, Thane and Raigarh. The community speak Urdu, but the Momin are bilingual, speaking Marathi as well. They are strictly endogamous, and tend to marry close kin. The Momin are Sunni, and are fairly orthodox community. Their traditional occupation was weaving, and many Momin have set up handlooms. Those Momin who have set up powerlooms tend to be more successful. Many Momin are employed by other Momin in these powerlooms, this especially is the case in the towns of Bhiwandi and Nagpur. A significant number of Momin are also employed in the textile industries. The Momin are largely an urban community, with only small number found as agriculturists. Many Momin are now successful entrepreneurs and professionals such as teachers, engineers and doctors. Like other Ansari communities, the Momin are members of the All-India Momin Conference, one of the oldest Muslim communal organizations in India. This organization acts as a welfare organization, as well as lobbying on behalf of the community." (Wikipedia)

Momin-Ansar Community

In India, the entire Momin-Ansari community has been identified as weaver's community, might be because a large section of the community mostly in the states of U.P., Bihar, Delhi, Maharashtra and Bengal are engaged in the occupation of weaving. They might have inherited the art of weaving from their forefathers who came to India from Yemen and other parts of Middle East (Detail in the chapter-'Origin of the Ansari community'). Though there is no historical evidence but there is also every likelihood that a section of the community might be convert from Hindu weavers called 'Tantis' and thus, inherited this art from them. Weaving, therefore, had all along been the mainstay of a section of this community since long and as such, somehow or another, the entire Momin-Ansar community has been identified as weavers community (*Bunker Biradri*). The affluent class of Muslims held themselves to be of superior class, self-classifying themselves as that of upper caste or 'Sharif' (noble) class and looked down upon their Muslim brethren belonging to occupational classes, classifying them as 'Razeel' (mean). This theory was make-believe for those of the occupational classes due to extreme illiteracy in ancient days. During earlier days of illiteracy amongst the Indian Muslim community, those belonging to occupational categories were called with derogatory names as '*julaha*' (weaver), '*dhunya*' (cotton carder), and 'kunjra' (vegetable grower) and so on. The word 'julaha' is in itself not derogatory which means a weaver. The word 'julaha' carries different theories. In Persian, *ZOOLA* means 'shuttle', an important accessory of the weaving loom. In ancient days, in India, the word Zoola was pronounced as *jula* and weavers were addressed as *Julaha*. Another fact is evident from the poem of Khaqani, a noted Persian poet, which says, '*Peisha-e-Ajdad Ma Julahgi Bawad*' meaning, 'profession of my forefathers was weaving (julahgi)'. In some other places in the Middle East and Arab world, it has been found that the word '*Julaha*' is used for those who weave fabrics. Somehow or another, it was found that only in Indian sub-continent, the word was used mainly by the self styled superiors as derogatory reference, not only confined to weavers, but for the entire Momin-Ansar community who were not in the profession of weaving.

Ansaris or the Momin community, according to the last census on caste basis held in the year 1931, comprised more than 65 per cent of the total Muslim population in India. They are spread over the entire country and their presence can be felt everywhere, in every city and the rural areas.

I started research on the issue few years back and met a cross section of the community. I have travelled extensively across the country and met Ansari families, both traditional weavers and artisans of wood carving in Saharanpur, those of the community engaged in glass work at Ferozabad and lock industry in Aligarh, carpet manufacturers of Bhadohi, Mirzapur, weavers of Delhi, Panipat, Mau, Varanasi, Tanda, Gorakhpur and a dozen of other places in Uttar Pradesh. Besides these professions, Momin-Ansaris could be found in other professions also.

Surnames

On the issue of fixation of different surnames by the members of the community, there had been some confusion and queries are often being put on the issue. The community affixes different caste surnames to their names, as- Ansari, Momin, Sheikh, etc. varying in different regions and areas of the country. In all the probabilities, this might be because the Momin-Ansari families in Bihar, U.P., M.P., Delhi, Haryana, Andhra, parts of West Bengal who commonly use 'Ansari' as surname, attribute it to the fact that since most of them are the offsprings of the generations of Hazrat Ayub Ansari who settled in different parts of the country, the surname of Ansari was derived from this parentage. It is worth noting that Ansaris from Medina moved to Gulf, Iran, Middle East, Afghanistan, Pakistan and India. However, Maulana Ashraf Ali Thanvi, the noted Islamic scholar who, for reasons best known to him only, was offensively biased against the Momin-Ansar community. The abusing words he used in his writings on this sensitive subject deserve to be slammed. This Maulana expressed his deep resentment against the Momin community for affixing the word Ansari to their names as in his narrow knowledge of sick mind it was sin to do so. God better knows which Islam he practiced, the *mukammal deen* based on Quran and Sunnah as left by holy prophet for his *Ummat* or the one full of mischievous innovations of Ulemas in this part of earth like Maulana Ashraf Ali Thanvi, Mufti Md. Shafi, Ahmad Raza Khan and their likes. Any innovation to the deen is simply bida't, a sin.

In Maharashtra, there is a divide. In that state, both 'Momin' and 'Shaikh' surnames are affixed. In Bhiwandi and Jalgaon 'Momin' is generally affixed as surname. There are two possibilities to affix the surname 'Momin'. In Arabic, 'Momin' word is generously used in the Holy Quran meaning thereby those Muslims with strong *Imaan* (faith). Since in India those of the Momin community were generally believed to be highly religious, this might be one reason. In this part of the country, offsprings of Momin Arif, a saint from Yemen who settled at Maner in the district of Patna, spread over in different parts, might be another possibility of Ansari community to be called as Momin community. In the history books, word Momin community has been widely mentioned. Apart from all these facts regarding different surnames of this particular caste, one thing is quite clear that in the part of the country comprising U.P., Bihar and Bengal where this movement was born, 'Momin' was identified with the organization. The organization was first named '*Jamiatul Momenin*' and later 'Momin Conference', which is now the house hold name in the community, quite familiar with the people of this country and the media besides Momin Conference has found its place in the pages of contemporary Indian history.

In some other parts surname of 'Shaikh' is commonly used. The general secretary of All India Momin Conference in fifties was an engineer, A. Sayeed Shaikh. In parts of West Bengal and Bihar, I found several Ansari families of earlier generations with the surname of 'Shaikh' not because of their desire to be called of upper caste but it was a traditional title coming from past generations. I could find that the earlier generations of the author himself, were with 'Shaikh' surname.

Apart from this practice, there are a large number of Ansari families who do not affix any caste surname. Some of the founders of the Momin movement and even a few of the past presidents of the Momin Conference were not identifiable with any such surnames. They included Maulvi Md. Yahya, Farkhund Ali, Shams Abdul Ghafoor, Md. Mohiuddin, Ali Ahmad Buland Akhtar, Maulana Imamuddin Ramnagri, Shamsul Ulema Maulana Mohammad Yahya, Qazi Abdul Jabbar, Asim Bihari, Sardar Latifur Rahman, Khan Bahadur Abdul Jalil, Khan Bahadur Mubarak Karim, R. Ali and a host of other top Momin leaders, besides Hafiz Shamshuddin, the president of the first Calcutta Momin Conference. Maulana Abdul Majeed Hariri and Md. Nezamuddin, Advocate, are all past presidents. A Muslim League stalwart and senior most leader of Bengal of pre-independent days was Raghib Ahsan. Though he came from the Momin-Ansar caste but did not use any surname. Likewise in Hyderabad, first cabinet minister of independent India was Ibrahim Ansari, but in contrast the General Secretary of All India Momin Conference, also from Hyderabad was Qasim Ali Abid. Apart from the facts mentioned, the media, especially the English media has picked up both Momin community and Ansari community for the community's references.

I am compiling this historical book in the fifteenth year of the 21st century. The flame of the movement was ignited in the beginning of the last century, though it took its formal shape in the year 1924.This movement, as a social organization, was then the need of the times to counter the age old taboo of caste system in the Muslim society which had acquired a menacing proposition. The evil of casteism in the Muslim society was the result of the hegemony of the haves coupled with the educational and social backwardness of the occupational section of the Muslim society. In those days, education and wealth were the domain of high and mighty, only. The evils of caste system in Muslim society had robbed those of the so-called backward castes of their rights to education. Taking undue advantage of this ground situation, the most disadvantaged class was exploited in so many ways and even held like slaves in certain areas. In short, the people belonging to the occupational classes were leading a miserable life.

A very long time has passed since then and a lot of water has flown down the rivers of the country. There is a vast palpable change of social and political chemistry of the country. India was a slave country at that time, now it is a sovereign nation. Educational backwardness and ignorance ruled over those people. After 1947, the nation has made remarkable strides and has gone to great heights. Education has enlightened the hearts and minds of the masses. And, so the behaviour of the people has also changed accordingly.

The caste system, though it cannot be genuinely claimed has altogether vanished from the Muslim society but, definitely, situation on this front has remarkably improved. There is more cohesion between different castes within the Muslim community and open caste-biased offensive is missing from the scene. There is now realization to the effect that Islam does not give credence to caste system thus inter-caste marriages, between so-called upper and lower castes, in the Muslim society are becoming common. Though, still there are families on both sides who prefer not to venture out of their own castes in marriage proposals.

Change is the rule of the nature. In this world, nothing is static. So is the case with different movements that sometimes created ripples in the lives of the people in different regions of the world and at different times, but with the passage of time, either became a part of the history or simply faded away. The strength of Communism has considerably dwindled and has lost its relevance in today's world. A century ago, the Indian National Congress created a storm against the British rule and dwarfed all the then conflicting ideologies before it. In a country of Hindu majority, the author of two-nation theory, Savarkar, alongwith the founders of RSS felt frustrated and had to nibble the grit before the secular tsunami spearheaded by Congress and for decades, before and after independence, the Hindutva movement failed to take off.

The movement of the Indian National Congress was so strong that ultimately the British government had to move out from this country. Today, Congress is gasping for life that has provided a chance for the Hindutva movement to take the centrestage of Indian polity.

The same rule of change has affected some prominent Muslim organizations also which were once landmark in India's history. The iconic figure behind Imarat Shariah that was established in 1929 as a religious cum political organization of Muslims of Bihar was Maulana Abul Mohasin Mohammad Sajjad. Its political outfit Muslim Independent Party won maximum of the 40 assembly seats under separate electorate during 1937 assembly elections. MIP was at the top when its nominee Md. Yunus was elected Chief Minister of the state for an interim period of two months. Maulana Sajjad died in 1940 after which its political organization faded away and became part of history.

After independence, All India Muslim Majlise Mushawarat was the most effective Muslim body that caused ripples in India's polity. In the seventy years old sovereign nation no other Muslim organization could come up to its stature. About three decades back, after the death of its president, Mufti Atiqur Rahman Usmani, Mushwarat was a divided house. It completely lost its relevance.

Renowned nationalist organisation of Ulemas, Jamiatul Ulema Hind, after the death of Maulana Asad Madni divided into two factions, one headed by his son, the other by his brother.

Momin movement is not an exception. After the death of Z.R. Ansari and that of his successor, Abdur Rauf Ansari just within a couple of years, Momin movement lost its dynamism. The nationalist body that scripted history and provided leadership to the Muslim community is itself in a bad shape. However, it is a matter of great solace that even today, there is a strong feeling in the Momin-Ansar community of India to infuse new life to the movement, for the good of the country and the community.

I am extremely thankful to all my admirers, well wishers and friends for their moral support and the encouragement they gave me to pen the history of Momin movement. For a long time, my friends in the Momin Community had been pressing hard to publish a most authentic book on this movement. Khalid Anwer Ansari, former state minister and illustrious son of Abdul Qaiyum Ansari, former Bihar minister and iconic figure of the movement, Fasihur

Rahman Ansari, son of Ziaur Rahman Ansari, former union minister and the tenth president of the All India Momin Conference, Prof. Humayun Morad, son of Nematullah Ansari of Gorakhpur and Manzoor Ahmad Ansari, son of Abdur Razzaque Ansari, former Bihar minister and distinguished Momin leader of Jharkhand were few who, all through, kept close contact with me and gave their moral support.

Some of the distinguished Muslim personalities, other than those from the Momin community, expressed their genuine desire for a comprehensive history on the movement. Maulana Anisur Rahman Qasmi, the Nazim of Imarat Shariah, Bihar, Jharkhand and Odisha topped the list. Throughout he remained a source of inspiration for me.

The present book will interest historians, scholars, researchers and will be of great value for those interested in minority politics. It should be a source of inspiration for the younger generations, too. The book will generate interest in the lovers of book and will be widely read.

A number of researchers from within and outside the country have already done researches on the movement. The latest to the list was Leislie Hempson from department of History, Michigan University, America. She was in Patna for quite a long period. She took advantage of this publication well before the formal printing process started.

Khurshid Anwar Arfi
kaarfi@rediffmail.com
Mobile: 91-9905812648

Introduction

Bihar has the distinction of being a fertile land that gave birth to a number of nationalist movements which blossomed to acquire a place of distinction in the pages of history. They played a decisive role in fighting against the barbarism of the British rulers on the Indian population. The Ulemas of Sadiquepore, a place in the eastern part of old Patna Township belonging to Ahle-Hadis school of Islamic thought, raised a banner of revolt against the imperial government and infused a strong sense of patriotism amongst the Muslim community. Tortured by the British government and imprisoned, they did not bend. They played a distinct role in the long struggle in dislodging the alien rulers. It is altogether a different matter that the ungrateful nation could not highlight the spirit of unadulterated nationalism of the Sadiquepore Ulemas that could have inspired the younger generations.

The Ulemas belonging to Deoband School of Islamic thought did not lag behind. A brainchild of Maulana Abul Mohasin Mohammad Sajjad of Nalanda district in Bihar and under the patronage of Maulana Abul Kalam Azad, Imarat Shariah was established at a national meet held at Pather-Ki-Masjid in east Patna in 1921 in the presence of distinguished Ulemas drawn from all over the country. Though, purely a religious but strictly a nationalist body, Imarat Shariah was all through in the centre of nationalist activities during the freedom struggle since nationalism and love with the country was the basic spirit of Islam. Maulana Sajjad, who was the president of Bihar Jamiat Ulema became Naeb Amire-Shariat. He floated Muslim Independent Party which contested first assembly elections in Bihar. The MIP got maximum number of seats out of that reserved for the Muslims in the first assembly elections on the basis of separate electorate in the year 1937. Before a regular government under Dr. Sri Krishna Sinha was formed, Md. Yunus, Advocate of the Muslim Independent Party was sworn in as the interim Chief Minister of the state for a couple of months.

Bihar is privileged by yet another nationalist movement, the Momin Conference, a nationalist organisation with its deep roots in Bihar, which created ripples in the Indian politics that played an unparallel role in the national freedom movement. It was unique in the sense that only one particular section within the Muslim community, the Momin-Ansaris, which formed the largest segment of the Muslim population of the country, rose united against the communal and separatist politics of the Muslim League. The peculiarity of the Momin movement was that the most economically, educationally and socially backward section of the Muslim community gathered courage to fight out centuries old un-Islamic practice of caste system amongst the Muslim community and dared to oppose the influential communal Muslim leadership confined to the elite section of the community, which was misguiding the Muslims in the name of separate homeland, thus, creating a divide between the two great communities of the land. The Momin community has always been of the strong view that the unity and integrity of this vast nation rests on communal harmony between two major communities, the Hindus and the Muslims, and any effort to destabilise this situation will bring disaster to the nation. The ideology practiced by the Momin Conference with exemplary courage and conviction made it to occupy a position on the top of Indian politics. Even sixty six years after the attainment of independence when the memory of the movement is gradually fading out, it is well preserved in the pages of history. The Indians of the last generation who are still surviving, vividly remember the ordeals of the Momin community at the hands of their Muslim brethren supporting Muslim League. The writer was himself a witness to an unfortunate incidence of the immoral behaviour of the Muslim League lampoons when in the heart of Patna town, Momin leaders were even denied food in Muslim restaurants. Even plates ready to be served with food were forcibly snatched, booed, jeered and driven out. They were branded *'Kafirs'* along with other non-Ansari Congress Muslim leaders for supporting Indian National Congress, in their opinion a 'Hindu party'. Since the Ansar-Momin community rejected the ideology of Muslim League and opted for the path of secularism as Congress did, the Muslim League leaders used to taunt the community being socially and economically weak, through this couplet of Akbar Allahabadi:

'Budhu Mian Bhi Hazrate Gandhi Kai Saath Hain: Hain Mushte-Khak Magar Aandhi Kai Saath Hain'.

The unprecedented nationalist upsurge among the Momin Community and its role in the national struggle for freedom has been admired by historians and leaders like Pandit Jawahar Lal Nehru. In his famed book, 'Discovery of India', Pandit Jawahar Lal Nehru wrote:

"The Momins, (principally, the weavers), though in large numbers, were the poorest and backward among the Muslims, and were weak and disorganized. They were friendly to Congress and opposed to Muslim League."

On another occasion, Pandit Nehru, in a letter addressed to Right Honourable Lord Pethic Lawrence, Secretary of State, India House, London wrote,

"Among the Muslims also, a fairly considerable movement arose among the Momins or the weavers class, which refused to associate with the Muslim League and was on the whole friendly to Congress and cooperated with it. They rejected the idea of Pakistan."

Wilfred Cantwell Smith, a social analyst commented in his book "Islam in India" on the role of the Momin Conference and wrote,

"The party *has been opposed to the League, Mr. Jinnah and Pakistan. It has been known for the self protection against the League......The Momin Conference's claim to represent millions of low caste Muslims, is probably valid."*

The barbarism and terror let loose on the weavers by the East India Company created a deep sense of hatred in their hearts against the British government. It was, therefore, quite natural that hatred against imperialism and spirited desire to end slavery was the strongest in the hearts and minds of the Momin Community.

Sense of Patriotism

Shaikh Bhikari

History will bear out the fact that right from the first war of independence in 1857 to the last battle in 1947, the Momin community was always there in the forefront. In Bihar when the banner of revolt was raised in the Ganges valley by Veer Kuer Singh, Martyr Shaikh Bhikari of the Momin community led the patriotic revolt against the British rule in the mountains of Chotanagpur. As the family story goes, Shaikh Lalu Budhan had a daughter, Amrit Bi and two sons. Shaikh Harkatullah was the elder son and Shaikh Bhikari was the younger. His original name was difficult to be pronounced by the tribals who called him Shaikh Bhikari and therefore, he was popularly known as Shaikh Bhikari. Shamima Khatoon Ansari wrote in her book in Urdu, 'Shaheed 'Shaikh Bhikari- Hayat Aur Khidmat' that Shaikh Bhikari was born at Hotappe in 1827. He commanded a very attractive personality. He was intelligent and since his childhood days, he showed his interest in swimming and archery in which art no body could beat him.

Shaikh Bhikari was the Deewan of Barka Ghar appointed by Thakur Wishwanath Shah Deo, Maharaja of Chotonagpur to look after his army at Barka Ghar. In the year 1857 inspired by Veer Kuer Singh and on the advice obtained from his minister, Pandey Ganpat Rai Deewan, Shaikh Bhikari decided to join the mutiny. The Indian regiment at Ramgarh killed their British officers. Nadir Ali Havildar and Ram Vijay Sipahi absconded to join the Army under Shaikh Bhikari at Jagannathpur. The mutiny took a serious turn and English men left Ranchi, Chaibasa and Santhal Pargana districts. Three Momin youths, Amanat Ali, Slamat and Shaikh

Heiro killed the English S.D.O. of Dumka. General Macdonald was after Shaikh Bhikari. He ultimately succeeded in arresting Bhikari and Umrao Singh on January 6, 1858. After a summary trial, both were hanged for treason and revolt on January 8, at Chatapalu Ghat. General Macdonald in his judgement wrote "Among the rebels, Shaikh Bhikari was the most dangerous mutineer."

It is irony that while memorials were set up and parks and buildings have been named after Veer Kuer Singh followed by official functions every year to remember the hero of Shahabad, Shaikh Bhikari's sacrifice has been totally ignored and forgotten by the establishment and he remained an unsung hero of the country.

Pir Md. Munis Ansari

A great revolutionary of the freedom movement and son of Phungan Mian, was born in 1882 in a middle class family of weaver's community Bettiah, Champaran in Bihar.

He was an eminent Hindi journalist and author. He wrote revolutionary articles in Hindi daily Pratap published from Kanpur. Pir Md. Munis Ansari was the first to highlight the sufferings of peasants of Champaran. He was known all over as the crusader for the rights of 19 lakh farmers. In 1917, he went to Allahabad to meet Pandit Sunder Lal, freedom fighter and author of "Two hundred years of British Rule". Here he met Ganesh Shankar Vidyarthi, the famed journalist also. He wanted that Congress should raise the issue with the government. However, both of them advised him that presently, he should continue to highlight the agony of farmers through his writings.

Secretary of Gandhi Memorial Committee, Motihari, Shri Brij Kishore Singh says that it is wrong to associate only the name of Ram Shukul with Champaran Satyagrah. In fact, Pir Munis was the real person behind. When Gandhi came to Champaran, Munis was all along with him.

Director of Jagjiwan Ram Research Institute, Sri Kant has said that during his research work, he could find in the book "Select document on Bihar visit of Mahatma Gandhi" written by B.B. Mishra that it was Pir Munis Ansari who was in the forefront in the efforts of bringing Gandhi to Champaran. Sheo Pujan Sahai has said that Ansari wanted to publish his collection of articles but were destroyed in earthquake. He further says that when Gandhi went to Champaran, he went to Ansari's house to meet his mother.

The Commissioner of Tirhut Division had in his report said that Pir Md. Munis Ansari was the first person who instigated people against the British government and second was Ram Shukul.

Shri Kant says that Professor Sajjad has started research work on Pir Md. Munis Ansari.

The road on which Pir Md. was living was named after him but after sometime, it was changed with the name of someone else.

Battakh Mian

Another notable person of the Momin Community was Battakh Mian, son of Md. Ali of Champaran who risked his job and even life to save the valuable life of Mahatma Gandhi. Battakh Mian was the Khansama in the British establishment at Motihari. In the year 1917, Mahatma Gandhi was scheduled to visit Motihari to personally asses the crisis faced by the farmers of Champaran. There was flutter in the district administration as they felt embarrassed with his visit. A conspiracy was hatched to physically eliminate Mahatma Gandhi during his stay there. Battakh Mian was taken into confidence and was conspired to mix poison in Gandhi's drink. Battakh Mian's conscience did not allow him to carry out the orders of his superiors and he decided to risk everything for saving the most valuable life of Gandhi.

Battakh Mian was a small entity, merely a Khansama but he did not care for his personal interest. If he would have carried out the orders from his British superiors, it would have been a different story for the nation. He not only saved a valuable life but saved the nation from the greatest catastrophe of the Indian history. Dr. Rajendra Prasad, the first President of Indian Republic appreciated the patriotic gesture of Battakh Mian. In 1950, when Dr. Rajendra Prasad visited Motihari, he could spot Battakh Mian. Dr. Prasad warmly embarrassed him. He ordered the district magistrate to take up official formalities to allot fifty acres of land to Battakh Mian in recognition of his taking up great risk to save the life of the father of the nation. But as the official machinery moves, the state government's attitude of dilly dally in the matter deprived Battakh Mian of this privilege.

{*At this point of my compilation, I was overwhelmed with emotions about the patriotic gesture of Battakh Mian to save the life of the Father of the Nation and in contrast, on another occasion, his gruesome murder by a fascist from his own community. Battakh Mian, the lowly paid staff of the British government risked his service and life to save the Mahatma and on the other hand, Nathu Ram Vinayak Godse, driven by the ideology of communal hatred, eliminated Mahatma Gandhi in a cold blooded murder. What a glaring example of patriotism and treason and a piece of par excellence that made a rich history. Sixty six years on, the ungrateful nation has forgotten Gandhi's Ahimsa and shamelessly embarrassed the ideology of hatred very much visible in Indian politics today.*— Author}

Brigadier Mohammad Usman

The Momin-Ansar community should be genuinely proud of its great son Brig. Md. Usman or Usman Mohammad. More so, since he was the highest ranking officer of Indian Army killed in the Indo-Pak war of 1947, who as a Muslim became a symbol of India's "inclusive secularism". He was awarded the Indian Army honour 'Maha Vir Chakra' posthumously.

Love for his mother land and patriotism has been described by the renowned Indian Journalist Khwaja Ahmad Abbas in these words: "a precious life of imagination and unserving patriotism, has fallen a victim to communal fanaticism. Brigadier Usman's brave example will be a abiding source of inspiration for the nation."

Brigadier Usman was born in the year 1912 in Bibipur, district Azamgarh, Uttar Pradesh. His mother was Jamilan Bibi, daughter of Abdul Kabir Ansari of Yusufpur. His father was Mohammad Farooque Khunambir of Bibipur. He was Shaher Kotwal Benaras. Usman was educated at Harish Chandra High School in Varanasi. He joined the Royal Military Academy at Sandhurst. In March 1935, he was appointed in the Indian Army and posted in the 5th battalion of Balluch Regiment. He was promoted to the rank of Lieutenant on April 30, 1936 and Captain on August 31, 1941.By April 1944, he was a temporary Major. He served in Burma and was mentioned in despatches as a temporary Major in London Gazette of September 27, 1945. He commanded the 14th Battalion of 10th Balluch Regiment from April 1945 to 1946. He was promoted to Major on August 31, 1946.

After partition, he refused to opt for Pakistan and turned down Pakistan's offer for Commander-in-Chief of Pakistan Army and preferred to continue to serve in India. He was transferred from Balluch Regiment to Dogra Regiment.

Captain Mateen Ahmed Ansari

Captain Mateen Ahmed Ansari GC of the 5th Battalion, 7th Rajput Regiment, in the Indian Army during World War II, and member of the British Army Aid Group, was awarded the George Cross posthumously. The decoration, the highest British (and Commonwealth) award for bravery out of combat, was announced in a supplement to the London Gazette of 16 April 1946 as being awarded for the 'most conspicuous gallantry.'

He was taken prisoner by the Japanese after they invaded Hong Kong in December 1941. After the Japanese discovered that he was related to the ruler of one of the Princely States they demanded that he renounce his allegiance to the British and foment discontent in the ranks of Indian prisoners in the prison camps. He refused and was thrown into the notorious Stanley Jail in May 1942 where he was starved and brutalised. When he remained firm in his allegiance to the British on his return to the prison camps he was again incarcerated in Stanley Jail where he was starved and tortured for five months. He was then returned to the original camp, where he continued in his allegiance to the British, and even helped to organise escape attempts by other prisoners. He was sentenced to death, with over thirty other British, Chinese and Indian prisoners and beheaded on 20 October 1943. He is buried in Stanley Military Cemetery in Hong Kong.

The patriotic fervor with which the entire Momin community participated at the initial stages of freedom movement was described by the District Gazettteer, Ghazipur in these words: "the most bigoted of all Musalmans" a favourable though biased assessment formed in the aftermath of the 1857 mutiny and quite obviously influenced by their active participation in the revolt".

Momin Conference was launched primarily, as a social organization to spouse the cause of the Ansari community in the year 1928 and to bring about consciousness amongst the Indian Muslims against the centuries old un-Islamic practice of caste system in India. Later, in response to the growing political need of the country, it was converted into a political party in the year 1939. It occupies a place of pride in the annals of contemporary Indian history. In close cooperation with the Indian National Congress, it played amazingly decisive role in the freedom movement and scripted a history, difficult for the nation to ignore. History of India's struggle for freedom will be incomplete without mentioning the role played by the Momin-Ansar community from the platform of Momin Conference. Historians and researchers have extensively recorded this movement in their works. The latest to be mentioned is the book, 'Community and Nations' authored by the slain historian and Professor of History, Patna University, Papiya Ghosh. She wrote "When Mr. M.A. Jinnah declared in Lahore session of the Muslim League that Indian Muslims were entirely behind his party, a very strong voice rose from Bihar where Mr. A.Q. Ansari trashed his claim and declared that the Ansari community was deadly opposed to communal politics of elite Muslims and "three crores of Ansaris" were entirely at the back of the Indian National Congress with their secular' credentials".

Congress Apathy

The towering Ansari leaders of the country, Dr. Mukhtar Ahmad Ansari (1880-1936) and Abdul Qaiyum Ansari (1905-1973) were strong pillars of secularism who gave unflinching support to the Indian National Congress in its fight against communal politics and did a great service to the nation. However, on its part, the Indian National Congress, which received valuable support during its very difficult days of freedom struggle from the Momin-Ansar community, chose to undermine its historical contribution to the freedom movement. It is unfortunate that Congress did not bother even to mention the strategic and materialistic support of the Momin Conference and its leaders to the party during its centenary celebrations. The Congress party has lately ignored the most deserving section of the Muslim community in its political scheme of things. This attitude of the Congress government towards the towering Muslim personalities of the country should be viewed in the backdrop of the liberal practice to raise memorials indiscriminately. In all the towns and cities anywhere in the country, one will find menacing installations of statues of political leaders. But you will not find a single statue of any leader belonging to the Muslim community which is bound to give a wrong impression on the minds of the younger generations. The Indian National Congress owes explanation for this blatant discrimination based on communal bias. An excuse is generally placed by those who are in power that in Islam, installation of statue is prohibited. For those who oppose or just take an excuse on this point should knwow that in the campus of Jamia Millia Islamia, quite visible to the naked eye from the passing road is the statue of Mirza Ghalib. There was no Muslim agitation against it. Yet on another prominent place in Delhi on the front of 'Krishi Bhawan', a big statue of Rafi Ahmad Qidwai is installed and another that of Asaf Ali at the Delhi Gate. Muslims never objected to it. However, it is true that generally installation of statues is not liked by a section of the Muslim community but the government has taken it as an alibi. The government could have taken alternate measures to erect memorials or rename important government institutions, buildings and airports etc. It seems that there is an undeclared policy of the government to suppress the role of the Indian Muslims in the freedom movement. Towns and cities are now menacingly flooded by such memorials. Universities, airports, other government buildings, parks, etc. have been named after leaders. In the first few years after independence when the country was being governed by leaders with 'genuine' secular credentials, they saw to it that in this process, communal bias against Muslim personalities was not practiced. Later, things started to deteriorate on this score.

Think of the unprecedented and rare contribution of these two leaders coming from the Momin-Ansar community. One will be genuinely shocked to know that the small stretch of road in Daryagunj, Delhi on which Dr. Mukhtar Ahmad Ansari's now dilapidated residential house, 'Darus Salam' stands and which was once a centre of political activities of top Congress leaders of the country during British raj, has been named 'Ansari Marg'. This was the only tribute to the great leader who deserved much more. On May 14, 1936, Asaf Ali proposed before Gandhi a befitting memorial in the name of Dr. Mukhtar Ahmad Ansari who had dedicated his services for the national movement. Asaf Ali was of the view that since Dr. Ansari was deeply involved in medical mission, the medical relief meant for the rural areas be named officially as 'Ansari Travelling Dyspensary' or 'Ansari Rural

Medical Corps'. But Gandhi did not take any notice of the suggestion made by Asif Ali.

A.Q. Ansari, who died in harness as a cabinet minister, could not yet deserve a befitting memorial, the man who dared to contest the claim of the Muslim League was the sole representative of Indian Muslims and hit back that the vast Momin community was secular and entirely with the Congress party. For his stand, Ansari and his followers had to face many ordeals at the hands of Muslim League volunteers. The way the Congress governments have ignored Momin luminaries from Shaheed Bhikari and Battakh Mian to Dr. Mukhtar Ahmad Ansari and Abdul Qaiyum Ansari is a sad story. Ansari was the tallest leader of the state. He joined the first elected state government in Bihar after independence as a cabinet minister. At least three of the most junior Congress leaders were nominated to head the state government in the state, totally ignoring Ansari's claim. However, Nitish Kumar showed a bit of his generosity and fairness when he ordered to include the name of A.Q. Ansari in the list of a number of departed leaders for official observance of birthdays as a mark of respect to the leader. An auditorium in Mr. A.Q. Ansari's name along with that of Maulana Mazharul Haque and Urdu journalist Ghulam Sarwar has also come up on the Hardinge Road of Patna besides the Haj Bhawan. This is certainly a bit of consolation for the Ansari community though still far less than what A.Q. Ansari really deserved.

Chandra Sekhar Singh

Apart from the failure of the Congress government to give proper recognition to these leaders, the Momins as a community was also denied of any special government privilege and scheme which could have helped it in educational and economic emancipation. Mr. A.Q. Ansari's continued sincere efforts for a long period to see that the Ansari community in Bihar could be favoured with Annexure 1 category, could not bear fruit as on every such occasion, the successive chief ministers turned down his plea. This attitude of the Congress Chief Ministers of his state was shocking for Ansari as the Momin-Ansar community deserved it the most. However the Momin community of Bihar is genuinely indebted to Chandra Sekhar Singh who, years after the death of Ansari, took over as the Chief Minister of the state. He had great admiration for the Momin-

Ansar community for its strong nationalist and secular outlook and heroic participation in the freedom movement. He was the one leader who generously praised the role of the Momin community in his speeches and used to thunder *"Momin biradri nai is desh ko bahut kuch diya hai kuch liya nahin"* (the Ansari community sacrificed for the nation but could never derive any benefit from it).

Chandra Sekhar Singh was always eager to help the community in a befitting manner. When he knew about the unsuccessful efforts of A.Q. Ansari to get the Ansari community in the Annexure 1 group, he expressed his strong determination to fulfill Ansari's dream. Though, he was competent enough to do the needful as the chief minister but he wanted to have a formal nod from General Secretary, Rajiv Gandhi and Prime Minister Indira Gandhi. Indira Gandhi had a deep knowledge about the Momin movement, its secular credentials and its role in freedom movement. She knew almost all the top Momin leaders. But Rajiv Gandhi did not have the knowledge of the movement. Chandra Sekhar Singh took pains to present Rajiv Gandhi a well drafted note about Momin community and its role. Later, he invited Rajiv Gandhi to attend a mammoth rally of the Momin community at the sprawling Gandhi Maidan in Patna which we had painstakingly organized. Chandra Sekhar Singh in his welcome address declared that his government was committed to put Momin community of Bihar in Annexure 1, which it deserved the most. Rajiv Gandhi formally endorsed his decision as the right step.

Chandra Sekhar Singh took several steps for the economic emancipation of the weavers of Bihar. The Momin leaders, A.Q. Ansari and Abul Ahad Mohammad Noor, being Chairman and Secretary, respectively of the society for Bihar Handloom weavers had purchased a big chunk of land at a prime place in Patna for the construction of its building. However, no construction work could be carried out for almost two decades because of lack of funds. The Handloom Union was in complete financial crisis due to mismanagement. However, Chandra Sekhar Singh was so impatient to help the handloom industry that he could not afford to wait for long. He knew that after he is dethroned, none will take any interest on that score. He saw to it that all hurdles in providing fund were cleared and took no time in laying the foundation of the 'Handloom Bhawan'. He nominated former minister, Hafiz Idris Ansari and me as the Chairman and Dy. Chairman of the Union and provided financial assistance out of the way. The Chief Minister, Chander Sekhar Singh was happy to lay the foundation stone on the western end of the plot where the commercial building, a part of Handloom Bhawan stands today. It was a festive occasion for the weavers community who attended in large numbers. Even the small section of the Momin community in the State Congress opposed to Chandra Sekhar Singh was morally forced to be present on the occasion. The majestic building standing magnificently in Rajendra Nagar is entirely indebted to the sincerity of Chandra Sekhar Singh. The weavers community of Bihar is grateful to Chandra Sekhar Singh whose strong political will could only make possible such a grand Handloom Bhawan, a reality. However, it is highly regrettable that with the political change of guards in the state and when the entire building was ready for formal inauguration, people were stunned to find that the stone slab symbolizing foundation laying by Chandra Sekhar Singh was missing. Whoever might be behind this shameful act, it has put the weavers community of Bihar highly embarrassed.

Chandra Sekhar Singh rewarded the Momin community politically also, which it deserved the most, during his regime. In parliamentary elections, he gave Congress ticket to Professor Md. Salahuddin to contest from Godda constituency. Salahuddin is the son of one of the stalwarts of the Momin movement, Md. Yasin Ansari of Santhal Pargana. He saw to it that Salahuddin wins the election. He campaigned vigorously to get him elected. In the assembly elections too, he eagerly searched a candidate for Sitamarhi constituency. He discussed the matter with us, took our opinion. Md. Khalil Ansari, a teacher serving in a primary school in Patna was the final selection who won the seat. He also nominated Abdur Razaqque Ansari of Irba, Ranchi in the Legislative Council.

Dr. A.R. Kidwai

Presently, Dr. Akhlaqur Rahman Kidwai, in late nineties, is on the top of the list of most outstanding Muslim personalities of the country. Dr. Kidwai is a scholar of repute. He was elected Chancellor of Aligarh Muslim University. Later he was appointed, first as a member then the Chairman of Union Public Service Commission for a record period of fourteen years. He was awarded Padma Vibhushan award in 2011.

Dr. Kidwai was the Governor of Bihar for over two terms and then he moved to occupy Calcutta Raj Bhawan. He was nominated Governor of Haryana and Rajasthan. He was nominated to Rajya Sabha also. With such a rich credentials to his credit, he is soft spoken and a perfect gentleman.

Hailing from Uttar Pradesh, Dr. Kidwai knew the Momin movement closely since pre-independence days. Like Bengal and Bihar, U.P. was the citadel of the movement. The patriotic gesture and the deep involvement of the Momin-Ansaris in freedom movement with a deep sense of sacrifice for the nation had very much impressed Dr. Kidwai. He was always ready to help genuinely the weaver's community. During his eleven years stay in Bihar, he kept himself closely in contact with the activities of the Bihar Momin Conference. He would often ring me with some new idea to boost the handloom industry in Bihar. Highly inspired by his deep interest and out of his initiative, we had arranged a number of meetings under the banner of Momin conference all over the state. Dr. Kidwai attended Biharshrif, Dhanbad and Ranchi conferences. He was deeply interested in the development of handloom industry in the state.

Once it so happened that Bihar was under a short spell of President's rule. It was the last day of the financial year. The Managing Director of the Bihar State Handloom Cooperative Union, Mr. Mishra came to me and said that the finance commissioner has turned down our request and was not willing to pass the bills of the Handloom Union. It was the last day and if bills were not passed, handloom weavers all over the state would suffer. I made a SOS call to Dr. Kidwai to convey him the seriousness of the matter. He immediately called his adviser to convey to the finance commissioner that if Handloom Weaver's Union bills were left out and not passed this financial year, meaning the same day, he will be sacked. This caused tremor in the finance department. The same finance commissioner took personal interest to see that the bills were passed by midnight under his supervision. Not only that, the finance commissioner saw to it that the related bills of the Union Textile Ministry lying for long were also cleared to the great relief to the poor weavers of the cooperative fold.

In the state of Jharkhand, Dr. Kidwai took keen interest in setting up a Weaver's hospital in memory of the Momin leader of Jharkhand, Abdur Razzaque Ansari at Irba of the standard of

Apollo hospital. The majestic building of the hospital stands on the main Ranchi-Patna highway. This was how Dr. Kidwai genuinely helped the weavers of the state.

Being governor of the state, he was also the Chancellor of all the universities. Since it was his prerogative to appoint Vice-Chancellors, Pro-Vice-Chancellors and Registrars, he felt that while different sections of people-, both from Hindu and Muslim communities approach him for favour but none from the Ansari community ever approached him for any such appointment. Once he called me and asked me whether the retired ADMs of Ansari community are interested in appointment as Registrar of University and if yes, bring them with their bio-datas.

I closely knew two persons, one Mozaffar Hussain and another A.R. Ansari. I rang them and told them all about. They were overwhelmed. By evening, both of them came with their bio-datas. Next day, I took them to Raj Bhawan. Dr. Kidwai took their brief interview and within one week, both of them received their appointment letters from Chancellor's office. Mozaffar Hussain was appointed Registrar of J.P. University and A.R. Ansari of S.K. University, now in Jharkhand.

Evil of Caste System

The majority community of India the Hindus, had, through centuries, made its deep impact on the cultural-religious lives of the Indian Muslims. The purity of Islam and its teachings coming down from Saudi Arabia, were diluted to a great extent in the Indian sub-continent under the influence of Hinduism that is very much palpable in the socio-religious lives of the Muslim community which continues till date. While Islam does not give credence to caste system, it has been very much in practice for centuries amongst the Indian Muslims. The continued hatred in the Hindu society against the backwards and the Dalits by the upper caste was to some extent visible in Muslim society too.

Teaching of Islam is quite clear on this issue. The holy Quran does not accept superiority of one individual on another on the basis of race, region or colour. Fraternity and equality (*Akhoowat & Musawa'at*) among the individuals is the basic creed of Islam. Only those Muslims, who are pious, fearful to Allah (*TAQWA*) and are in full submission to Him, stand superior in the eyes of the almighty. The teaching of Islam in this respect was demonstrated by Prophet Mohammad who honoured the slave of Habsha, Hazrat Belal appointing him as the first Moazzin (caller for prayer). Our prophet nominated Zaid-bin-Harsa, a slave as the commander of army (Amir of Lashkar) and later his son, Osama bin Zaid to the post. He preferred a slave against a Quraish of Mecca. After Prophet's death, first caliph (Khalifa-e-Awwal) Hazrat Abu Baker Siddique respected the wishes of Prophet Mohammad and allowed Osama bin Zaid to continue as commander. During army march, Osama bin Zaid rode on the camel back being the commander and even the Caliph Abu Baker marched on foot. Not only that, at one point Abu Baker begged excuse and wanted permission to leave for very urgent discussions with Umer bin Khattab. This was the essence of humanity and discipline Islam taught. Hadith says that Prophet Mohammed used to keep slaves closer to himself. How dear *'Akhoowat' and 'Musawat'* are to All'ah Subhanahu Ta'alaa and Prophet Mohammad that reflected in the lines of the poem of Allama Dr. Iqbal:

> *Ek Hi Saf Mein Kharai Ho Gai Mahmood-o-Ayaz*
> *Na Koi Banda Raha Aur Na Koi Banda Nawaz*
> *Banda-o, Saheb-o, Muhtaaj-o-Ghani Ek Huai*
> *Terai Darbar Mein Ponhchai to Sabhi Ek Huai*

Prophet Mohammed told his Umma before death that the *Deen-e-Islam* was complete and warned that hereafter, nothing should be added to Quran and Sunnah which will amount to innovation (Bida't). There is a Hadith to that effect. On the authority of Abu Najah-al-Irbad bin Sina which was related by Abu Dawood and Al-Tirmidih who said that it was a good and sound Hadith. It is as follows:

> *"Beware of newly invented matters, for every invented matter is an innovation and every innovation is going astray: and every going astray is in hell fire."*

Notwithstanding the teachings of Islam, in the Indian subcontinent, it was mere hegemony of the self appointed guardians of Islam, the rich and the educated, the Jagirdars, Nawabs and Zamindars, though, numerically in minority but socially and economically powerful, self-placed themselves in the category of upper caste and all those sections of Muslims who earned their livelihood through their skill and hard labour (occupational class), were considered a discredited lot and looked down upon. For their selfish interest, the haves in the Muslim society found it convenient to ignore the teachings of Islam and treaded the path of Hindu religion. They exploited the have nots for their own benefits and taking advantage of their economic superiority meted out inhuman treatment to the so-called low caste Muslims. The Ansaris, who constitute the largest segment of the Muslim population, were a highly demoralized lot. They were made sick of inferiority complex. Socially, educationally and economically downtrodden,

Ansaris were looked down upon, harassed, humiliated and oppressed by a section of their own community and called them with bad and derogatory names. They picked up the word *'Julaha'* to address the Ansaris only to tease and humiliate them. Islam gives a place of honour and dignity to weavers and artisans and all those of the occupational classes that is reflected in authentic Hadith, *'Kasb Habibullah'*. Mullah Jiwan, the author of famous work on principle of Hadith and Fiqah, *'Nurul Ala Noor'* came from a weaver's family. Not only that, in the house of Imam Abu Hanifa, he had a flourishing business of cloth weaving. Prophet's companion (Sahaba), Hazrat Ayub Ansari and Hazrat Talha Ansari, another Sahaba, were weavers. Entirely ignoring these historical facts, it is irony that even some Islamic scholars in this subcontinent wishfully ignored these basic teachings of Islam and came out with unconvincing and mischievous interpretations of the teachings of the holy Quran to support the taboo of caste system smuggled into the Muslim society.

There is no historical evidence, as maliciously claimed by a section of the self styled *'Shareef'* class of the Muslim society and advocates of caste system in Islam, that Ansaris were converts from *'Shudras'*. This was just a concocted theory adopted to suit them and can only be termed as the 'mischievous theory of convenience'. The historical facts dispel such a theory which maliciously meant to keep the Indian Muslims divided through centuries and therefore, deserves to be trashed. Can those who are in the habit to mischievously propagate such absurdity could ever produce authentic historical fact to prove their logic?

Tracing back to the origin of human history, when Adam and Eve descended on the earth planet, their foremost requirements were those of food and clothing. Thus from day one of the human presence on earth, the arts of agriculture and weaving acquired importance and respectability which continues till date. Adam was the first weaver. Gabriel (Hazrat Gibrael, the Angel) taught the art of weaving to Adam. Shah Abdul Aziz in his book *'Fathul Aziz'* referring to a Hadith says that Adam had first woven three pieces of cloth, one for himself, another for Eve (Bibi Hawwa) and third, a chadar to cover both of them. Adam trained his son Sheish who did weaving for 444 years. Prophets Hazrat Zakaria (Zechariah) and Hazrat Nooh (Noah) were engaged in the profession of carpentry, Hazrat Idris was a tailor, Hazrat Ibrahim

(Abraham) did agriculture work, Hazrat Sulaiman (Solomon) made fan and basket from dried tree leaves, Hazrat Isa (Christ) used to sell yarn spun by her mother Bibi Maryam (Mary) in their house and the first caliph (*Khalifa-e-Awwal*), Hazrat Abu Bakar Siddique had a flourishing business of textile weaving. Another renowned companion of Prophet Mohammad, Abu Talha Ansari was also a weaver by profession. Going through the Islamic history, one finds that quite a number of prophets were engaged in occupational works like carpentry, tailoring and other professions. Quotes from Hadith indicate that Prophet Mohammad once said that there was no such prophet who had not done grazing of goats. In response to another question, he said yes, earlier he also earned by grazing goat.

Maulana Hussain Ahmad Madni in his autobiography '*Naqsh-e-Hayat*' has written pages after pages against the evil practice of caste system, very much against teaching and the basic spirit of Islam in the Indian sub-continent. He writes....

"though Abu Lahab, Abu Jehal and Valeed who were exalted members of Quraish-e-Makka could not get even fraction of the honour what Hazrat Belal, Hazrat Sulaiman and Hazrat Suhaib could get from Prophet Mohammad. In the same way due to his sincerity and sacrifices, Abu Baker Siddique, first caliph was buried by the side of the prophet. It was a great honour. But Hazrat Abbas and Hazrat Ali, though they were so closely related to Prophet Mohammad, could not get this honour. Hazrat Maulana Hussain Ahmad Madni wrote that the evil of false racial pride among Muslims is mostly in India due to the social effect of Hindus and Islam is deadly opposed to such practice."

Writing about his own racial status, Maulana writes, '....My father during the period he was the headmaster posted in Safipur, Bangar Mau, District Unnao (U.P.), when used to tell people that he belonged to Tanda and was from a family of Syed and peerzadas, people won't believe his words because Tanda was a place inhabited by handloom weavers. They generally believed that we were also from among them....'

Maulana Ekhlaque Hussain Qasmi, an Islamic scholar expressed his opinion about the practice of caste system in Indian sub-continent and the dignity of labour in Islam in his article in Urdu, '*Sanat-o-Hirfat*' in a souvenir published in 1994. Quoting several examples from Islamic history, Maulana Qasmi said that companions *(Sahabas)* of Prophet Mohammad (pboh) used to construct their mud houses with their own hands. Even Prophet Mohammad, like a labourer, worked in the construction of the first mosque, Masjid-e-Aqaba'. He used to carry stone slabs for the construction of its walls. Wife of Prophet Mohammad, Hazrat Bibi Zainab used to tan animal skins and from her earnings, she will purchase honey for her husband. He stressed that in Islam all through during fourteen hundred years, nowhere in the Islamic world, ever existed any system of upper and lower division based on occupation, nor is today, except in the Indian sub-continent. Maulana further emphasised that Prophet Mohammad always held that there is dignity of labour bestowed in Islam and had said that *Alla'h Subhanahu-Ta'ala* loved persons who earns through labour. However, he says that all those who came as warriors through Khaiber pass were totally different from those who came and settled from Arab. They badly suffered from wrong notions and for their own convenience and strategical governing benefits, embraced the practice of caste system already prevalent in the Hindu society.

The noted Urdu novelist-journalist of yester-years Khawja Ahmad Abbas was a columnist of R.K. Karanjia's most famous magazine 'Weekly Blitz' (now seized publication) being published in Urdu, Hindi and English. In his regular 'Last Page' column, Khawja Ahmad Abbas wrote, "It is only in this subcontinent that dignity of labour is abused. Those who, day in and day out, laboured hard to earn their livelihood, are looked down upon and have placed them at the most lower level 'Razeel' in the society. This class was made to suffer and was leading a wretched life of depravity in the society. But those who exploited the occupational classes and enjoyed the fruits of their labour, suffered from the false notion of being superior '*Sharif*' class. How ridiculous is that!'

There is certainly no evidence of such classification in the divine words of *Allah Subhanu-Ta'ala or Hadith*. Those who suffered from false complex of superiority, in fact do not respect the 'dignity of labour' enshrined in the teachings of Islam. In today's modern world, 'Dignity of Labour' is widely talked about but more than fourteen hundred years ago, it was the basic point in the teachings of Islam".

The most unfortunate aspect of this sad story was that a small section of the clerics (theologians), the Ulemas and the Muftis, who are supposed to be the guardians of Islam, not only failed to protect the most distinct and honoured feature of equality, dignity and brotherhood (*Islami Akhoowat*) that makes Islam different from any other religion, instead they fell in line and willfully embraced and even practiced the un-Islamic caste system. Some Islamic scholars in this subcontinent dared to ignore and came out with unconvincing and mischievous interpretations of the teachings of the holy Quran to support the taboo of caste system smuggled in the Muslim society. To bring home their point, they cleverly rested their argument on Quranic word *'Kuffu'* which means equality of social status. Misinterpreting *'Kuffu'* maliciously, they even issued 'Fatwa' calling upon the so-called upper caste Muslims not to give their children in marriage to those of the Ansari community and other such professional castes on the basis of *'kuffu'*. How ridiculous it was!

The worst came from Mufti Mohammad Shafi of Deoband, who in his book, *'Ghayatun Nasab'* made humiliating and derogatory remarks against the profession of weaving and on that score, the Ansari-Momin community contradictory to *'Al' Kasib Habibullah'* encouraged caste system among the Muslims. He was so aggressively biased against the weaver community that he wrote *"in julahoon nai teen waqt ki nemaz kiya ada kar li kai apne aap ko jannati samajhnei lag*ai." There was turmoil in the campus on the issue. Maulana Mohammad Usman, founder of *'Jamiat-Al-Salehaat'* who was then a student of Darul Uloom, rose against the un-Islamic contention of Mufti Shafi. The great Islamic scholar Mufti-e-Azam Hind, Mufti Kifaetullah and Sheikhul Islam Hazrat Maulana Hussain Ahmad Madni along with other Ulemas of different school of thought were all unanimous to ridicule Mufti Shafi, trashed his views with contempt it deserved and blamed Mufti Shafi for presenting Islam in bad light. Mufti Kifaetullah had to issue fatwa against Mufti Shafi's views. Whatever reputation Mufti Shafi had gained as a most distinguished Islamic scholar and for his services to furtherance the cause of Islam were all washed away and he became a sore even in the eyes of Islamic scholars. His book was ultimately banned and in disgust, the controversial Mufti found an escape in crossing over to Pakistan.

Despite the teaching of Islam regarding *Akhoowat* and *Musawaa*t and Prophet Mohammad's stress on the dignity of labour, so dear to *Alla'h Subhanahu Ta'ala,* prominent Indian theologians,

Maulana Ashraf Ali Thanvi, Maulana Ahmad Raza Khan and alike have brazenly defying the holy Quran and Prophet Mohammad, shamelessly stooped low to malign the God fearing, low profile occupational class of Momin-Ansar caste with highly derogatory and dirty remarks.

Another luminary, Sir Syed Ahmad Khan, who is genuinely credited to bring about educational revolution amongst the Indian Muslims during that period, was suffering from the same mental make-up as that of Mufti Shafi. He was known pro-British and fell in the category of those Zamindars and Jagirdars who kept themselves away from the Indian mainstream of freedom struggle and openly sided with the British government for their selfish interest. Maulana Abul Kalam Azad too, appreciated Syed's educational mission but was apprehensive of his political views. In his book, *'Asbab-e-Baghawat-e-Hind'*, Sir Syed Ahmad Khan expressed his displeasure over the mutiny of 1857. Pointing his accusing finger towards the Momin-Ansar community in a most derogatory and uncultured manner, he wrote, "Yeh *Bad Zaat Julahai Baghawat Mein Pesh Pesh Thei*" (these mean-caste *Julahas* were in the forefront of the mutiny). Sir Syed meant to blame the community in a most derogatory manner and prove its disloyality to the British government but in fact, it proved to be a blessing in disguise as the nationalist role of the community was beyond any doubt.

The fact cannot be denied that it were the Muftis, Mashaekhs Mujtahids and Ulemas, infested with the virus of casteism, who had done greatest disservice to Islam by giving credence to cast system and propagating it among the Indian Muslims, which is un-Islamic. They did what even non-believers could not do to defame Islam in the last centuries. They wrote articles, editorials and produced innumerable literature in the shape of monthlies, periodicals and books. Taking undue advantage of their religious learnings and positions acquired, in religious bodies, they tried their best to defame Islam in the sub-continent. It is they who have presented Islam in a mutilated form in India.

Contrary to that, there is an exhaustive list of a galaxy of most distinguished and top brass of Ulemas, past and present, who strongly condemned this trend. Among those—Maulana Mufti Kafaetullah gave innumerable *Fatwas* denouncing casteism in Islam. He published collection of *Fatwas, 'Kafaetul-Mufti'*. Maulana

Abul Kalam Azad wrote a book, *'Masaal-e-Kifaet'*. Sheikhul Hadees Hazrat Maulana Hussain Ahmad Madni was one person who was all out to defend the spirit of Islam. Maulana Habibur Rahman Azmi wrote, 'Tazkeratun-Nasajeen'. Jamiat Ulema-e-Hind under the presidentship in its eleventh (11th) session at Jaunpur in the year 1940 passed a strong worded resolution condemning the section of Ulemas who were spreading falsehood about casteism in Islam and accused them of dividing Indian Muslims. Again in its thirteenth (13th) session held at Lahore in the year 1942, Jamiat Ulema-e-Hind under his presidentship passed an exhaustive resolution on the un-Islamic custom of casteism on the pattern of Hindu brethren. The resolution declared that brotherhood among all sections was the bane of Islam and the most distinguishing feature amongst all other religions of the world. It also decried the behaviour of a section that, for personal ego, was misguiding Muslims. Prominent among those who attended the meet and fully supported the resolution included Maulana Abul Kalam Azad, Maulana Abdus Samad Rahmani, Maulana Syed Lutfullah Shah, Maulana Md. Tayyab, Mufti Atiqur Rahman Usmani, Maulana Mufti Kafaetullah, Maulana Shabir Ahmad Usmani Maulana Abdul Majid, and others.

The younger group amongst the Muslims also realized the disastrous effect of caste system that infiltrated in Islam in this part of the world and decided to wage a war against what they considered un-Islamic and against the teachings of Quran and Hadith. A few years back, they formed a body named Student Islamic Movement of India (SIMI). However, government has put ban for its alleged role in the act of terror.

Nematullah Ansari

During British rule, after the mutiny of 1857, the alien government went on a spree of 'divide and rule' policy between Hindus and Muslims and even within the two communities, as well. While there was popular and historical upsurge against the British Raj in the country, out of their strategy to unsuccessfully neutralize its effect, the Nawabs, Jagirdars and Zamindars were conferred with titles, with special powers, rested in Khan Saheb, Khan Bahadur and Rai Saheb and Rai Bahadur. A few were picked up from the Momin-Ansar community, also to be conferred with these titles who were in Muslim League. The British government had, it is said, also given powers to the superior class to collect taxes from the untouchables, the lower caste people of both the communities and other weaker sections in different forms.

Papiya Ghosh writes in her book, "Community and Nation", 'The '*Julahas*' who were of weaver descent were regarded as the lowest of the Muslim biradris and in many areas forced labour was taken from them freely. In Bihar, the zamindars of Gaya and Shahabad, for example, employed them as customary porters. An illegal tax, Kathiari was extracted on their handlooms by zamindars, also a monthly royalty on the net profit of each loom called masarfa. In many areas, the zamindars claimed an illegal house tax known as *ghardwari*.'

In a related story, in the city of Gorakhpur there lived a highly cultured and educated family of Nematullah Ansari. He was born in 1903 in Mohalla Ismaelpur in the city of Gorakhpur. His father Mianji Rahmatullah had a flourishing business spread over to U.P., Bihar and Bengal. In the biography of Nematullah Ansari, it is mentioned that Nurur Rahman, father of Banga Bandhu Shaikh Mujibur Rahman, worked for sometime in his handloom industry. Qazi Talmaz Hussain, the zamindar of Gorakhpur used to collect 'Ghardwari Tax' from the Ansari community. He demanded the same from Nematullah Ansari also who refused to pay the tax and decided to fight out the unfair and humiliating practice. Highly offended, Qauzi Talmaz Hussain went to the court of Munsif Magistrate with his prayer that Nematullah Ansari be directed to pay Rupees 5 and 4 Annas due with him as 'Ghardwari Tax'. His plea was that he was a Zamindar and had every right to collect 'Ghardwari Tax' from the low caste Muslims. This case of unprecedented nature created stir within the Muslim community. For the first time, one from the community Nematullah Ansari could gather courage to stand against the un-Islamic behaviour of the affluent section of the Muslim community and refused to pay the illegal tax. Lot of heat was generated and no efforts were spared on both sides to showdown each other. There was an unfortunate war of words and booklets like '*Julaha Nama*' and '*Qauzi Nama*' were distributed maligning each other. Mr. Istefa Hussain, who later became a minister after independence and Reyazuddin Ahmad, who was elected Deputy Speaker of U.P. assembly, advocated the case of Nematullah Ansari. The case was dismissed.

Qauzi went for appeal to the Allahabad High Court. A very brilliant Ansari advocate and M.L.A from Bihar, Khan Bahadur Abdul Jalil, offered to fight the case on behalf of Nematullah Ansari. The arguments in the case were confined whether Ansaris were 'mean' (Razeel) or 'noble' (Sharif). After a long debate, the learned judge held that the Momin-Ansar were not '*Razeel*' hence they were not obliged to pay the 'Ghardwari Tax' Humayun Morad, son of Nematullah Ansari is a retired professor of Aligarh Muslim University. He has since settled in Aligarh.

It was in this mutilated form that Islam in India then existed.

Atrocities on the Community

Wrong and deceptive notion of being superior, the so called '*Sharif*' among the Muslims were accused of unleashing atrocities on the Momin community. A number of cases were found in which the Zamindars took forced labour from the members of the poor Momin community. Narrations of oppression of the community were most common in Bihar and U.P. During that period, every meeting of the Momin Conference mainly dealt with this menacing problem. In Bihar, with strong Momin leadership, the issue was fought effectively and with determination. President of Champaran Momin Conference, Hafiz Din Mohammad addressing a meeting at Tappa Deoraj gave a detail account of 'un-Islamic' oppression of the Muslims by the elite Muslims. At Begusarai Momin Conference, A.A. Mohammad Noor catalogued the treatment meted out to his community. In Shahabad, Hafiz Manzoor Hussain quoted several instances of Momins being exploited by the Zamindars.

At the first Bihar Provincial Momin Conference, A.A. Mohammad Noor pointed out that ironically while the upper class Muslims in the past demanded a royal commission to inquire into their oppression by the Hindus, they seemed completely unmindful of the atrocities they had perpetrated on the so-called low caste Muslims.

An enquiry committee under the chairmanship of Dr. Aminuddin Ahmad of Biharsharif was formed for the purpose. During the course of inquiry, Dr. Ahmad made a statement about some Momins of village Deawaan, Islampur, district Patna being framed in false cases by the Muslim League President in retaliation to their refusal to leave the Momin movement and join League.

However, the myth of superiority over others was broken by Maulana Hakim Abul Hoda Abdus Salam Mubarakpuri, an assistant librarian in the Khuda Bakhsh Oriental Public Library at Patna. He wrote a book on the origin of the Momin-Ansari community, *'Tarikhul Minwal'* in Urdu. He had started a series of publications under the title of *'Al-Tamaddun'*. The second part of the book carried the title of *'Tarikhul Minwal-wa-Ahla'*.

It is a classical piece of excellent research work meticulously carried out on the subject. For the first time, the origin of the Momin community in India could come into light. This book was released the same year when Maulana Abul Kalam Azad's *'Al-Helal'* was published. Writing on the sensitive issue, Mubarakpuri took full advantage of the priceless treasure at the Khuda Bakhsh library on the subject that made the book highly authentic. This was the first book written on the subject. It created a stir in the Muslim community as the authors of the false conception of the 'smuggled' caste system in the Muslim community got fully exposed. There was lot of hue and cry over the publication by the affected quarters but the credibility of the book could not be challenged as it was based on rich and authentic quotations from the Islamic history written by distinguished writers including renowned historian Halim Sharar.

The book, *'Tarikhul Minwal'* is a rare commodity now. Mohiuddin, Bar-at-Law was so nice to gift the book to the author in all faith before he died. He wrote on the first page, "To, K.A. Arfi, who deserves entrustment of this treasure, with all my love, affection and best wishes" Mohiuddin, Tezpur (Assam) 5.7.79. (The author records with a deep sense of gratitude to Mr. Mohiuddin for this priceless gift.)

Atmosphere of Cordiality

The evil of caste system among Indian Muslims got a beating after independence. The defeat of the political ideology practiced by a large section of the Nawabs and Zamindars and subsequent abolition of Zamindari system in India brought a remarkable change in their mental attitude. They suddenly fell from the top to the rock bottom of their lives. Already demoralised with the partition of the country coupled with their economic bankruptcy as an after affect of Zamindari abolition, this particular section of the elite Muslims could no more afford to menace the Muslim society with false notion of superiority as they were themselves drawn into inferiority complex. Darkness engulfed their lives and their very survival, at one stage, was at stake. Those who till then considered themselves superior and far above the rest of the Muslim community and had strong reservations in mixing with other Muslims were now themselves facing social isolation. For example, in Bihar, the Patna city area of state capital was a cluster of Nawabs and Zamindars. While in Patna, I had the opportunity to watch with a mixed sense of sorrow and outrage their painful transformation from an affluent class to a wretched lot. In the passages of holy Qura'an, a Muslim reads about harrowing tales of divine curse on those who defied prophets and the teachings of *Allah SubhanauTa'ala* and embraced all sorts of evils. What I had learnt from holy Qura'an, I had the opportunity to watch the fate of those who blatantly defied the teachings of Qura'an and Hadith as the horrors of present day '*Saile-Iram*' was very much evident before my eyes in a new form. It was a story of a rich and affluent class of people who became penniless with the sudden turn of events. Those who once recklessly drove their Bueke, Ford or Austin dressed in spotless and choicest dresses on the roads of Patna were spotted on rickshaws and tongas that presented a sorrowful story of their miseries. It was a story of 'from riches to rags'. A very pathetic situation had overtaken and all sorts of social evils had crept into their lives, unspeakable, to the shame of the entire Muslim community.

Here is another related story that speaks a lot of the mindset that can only be described as false pride or '*Zoam-e-Batil*'. It is still very much fresh in my mind which I would like to share with my readers. Syed Jafar Imam, the flamboyant Muslim League State General Secretary turned Congress Minister in Bihar was a noble person. He had served Muslim League under the presidentship of its President S.M. Ismail, popularly known as Hajjan Nawab. He was a humorous person and very nice in gossips but with a bad mouth. He was a sensitive person too and was reasonably pained and distressed over the pitiful condition of this particular lot of Patna City as anybody else. He spoke to Abdul Qaiyum Ansari and Abul Ahad Mohammad Noor, two of his cabinet colleagues about the plight of those who were till the other day the most dignified persons of the Muslim society of Patna and used to a fabulous life. It was decided that they will meet at A.A.M. Noor's Serpentine Road residence to discuss the grave issue and plan way out for their honourable rehabilitation. Syed Jafar Imam narrated the horrors of their families with tears rolling down his cheeks. He was a sensitive man of high emotions. These stalwarts discussed a few solutions but were considered impractical. A.A.M. Noor came out with a solution which, in his opinion, the women folk could earn livelihood within the forewalls of their dwellings. He suggested that arrangements should be made to provide them with Charkhas to spin cotton yarn which will be, in turn, supplied to looms for production of fabrics. Syed Jafar Imam got enraged on the very proposal and found it humiliating for the Nawab families. He bluntly remarked that Noor Saheb now wanted that the families of the Nawabs should do the job of weavers, a mean job which was never acceptable. One can imagine the made out perception against the noble profession of weaving by the self styled '*Sharif*' of the muslim society. His false ego of being so called superior class was hurt and left the place in a huff.

However, over the years after independence, there has been sea change in both attitude and thinking, for the good, within the Muslim society. In the modern age of today when growing adoption of education in the community has enlightened the hearts and minds of young Muslims, there is serious realization that caste system in the Muslim society in older days was anti-Islamic. While the feudal system is now a story of the past, the present generation views the 'artificial' caste system as a curse for the Muslim society. The present generation of backward Muslims whose parents suffered these ordeals sincerely feel that, in their own interest and in the larger interest of the Muslim community of India, should forget and forgive. The bitterness between different castes that once dominated the society has to a great extent, if not totally, lessened and there is more cohesion and cordiality.

On the other side, after ushering in of democracy and with wider opportunities and better job avenues open, younger generation of the Momin-Ansar caste and also those of other occupational classes, started showing up in education and got success in civil and technical competitions. Boys and girls of the Momin-Ansar community have flooded the software industry, private banks and business institutions. Their efforts to qualify in state and Union civil examinations have proved fruitful. This led to a palpable change in the Muslim society which is reflected in the marriage ads coming up in newspapers in which 'no caste bar' is now being prominently displayed. Inter-caste marraiges among Muslims are becoming common now. A strong wave of changed mindset has taken over the Muslim community, specifically the younger generation, which refuses to give credence to caste system prevalent in the older days of illiteracy. To quote a few prominent cases: Ahmadullah Bukhari, Shahi Imam of Jama Masjid, Delhi is married to the daughter of Md. Yusuf Ansari, former five-time Member of Parliament from Siwan; youngest daughter of former Member of Parliament Syed Shahabuddin is married to the grand son of former D.I.G of Police, Bihar, A.R. Ansari and son of former Union Minister and B.P.C.C President, Rafique Alam is married to the youngest daughter of Md. Yusuf Ansari, ex-M.P. There are innumerable such cases. This is definitely a welcome sign that the evil of caste system is slowly fading away from the Indian Muslim society. Good senses have ultimately dawned upon and, in general, there is serious realisation to the effect that this false notion of older days of illiteracy that was common in the majority of the Muslim population, was now proving disastrous for themselves as due to strict caste limitations and dowry system in some families, it had become increasingly difficult to find a suitable match. As a result in considerable number of families, girls were getting overage and their marriage was becoming difficult. Presently, this is the harsh reality of the Indian Muslim society. However, unmindful of this scenario, there still exits a microscopic minority in the Muslim society suffering from false ego of being superior or of upper caste as they seem to be determined not to face the reality of the present times.

Arab Ancestry of Ansaris

It is a fascinating history of the ancestors of a branch of Ansaris in India who, few thousand years ago, started their journey from Yemen to Yasrab (Medina), to Constantinople (Istanbole) to Hirat and finally, to India. Ansaris are noble people as in Arab language Ansari means who helps others. They were valliant warriors and religious, too. They fought battles from Badar to Constantinople and did *'Tabligh'* wherever they went. They were first to accept Islam and had the distinct honour to host Prophet Mohammad at Medina when he took to *Hijrat* from Mecca. They came and settled in different parts of Indian sub-continent and made the countries (India, Bangladesh & Pakistan) their homes and never went back. Those who came to India as invaders, looted the wealth and went back. The Ansaris from Arab peninsula were attracted by the love of the people, their friendly behaviour and religious tolerance. They did not enter India with the intention to plunder but to make India their home. Since centuries, the Ansaris are in this country, generation after generation. They, whether from Arab ancestry or convert, are not bystanders. The Momin-Ansar among the Muslims of the sub-continent is of the most noble and distinguished class. They have contributed to religion, politics, medicine and made their presence felt in every sphere. Ansaris are considered highly religious mostly belonging to the Ahle-Hadis school of Islamic thought, secular in nature and patriot to the core. They are both Shia and Sunni, though Shia Ansaris are quite less in numbers and are confined in the Kashmir valley, Varanasi and in some areas of central U.P.

Islamic history throws sufficient light on the historical events that leads to strengthen the centuries old belief that a section of the Ansari community in India has roots in Arab and were the descendants of Hazrat Ayub Ansari. Most of the families of the

Momin-Ansar community simply knew this bare fact which came down from one generation to another, but there was no such document which could confirm this till researches in the light of Islamic history were made. However, here at home, Mufti Mohammad Shafi of Deoband, a prominent protagonist of caste system in Islam was upset to know about Ansaris Arab ancestry and wrote a book, *'Ghaetun-Nasab'* to denounce the 'courage' of the 'mean *Julahas'* to claim themselves to be from the generation of the most exalted companion of Hazrat Mohammad (PBUH), Ayub Ansari. It hurt the ego of Mufti Mohammad Shafi who symbolized the section of Muslims who dared to overrule the teachings of Quran and Sunnah and harped on self created *Sharif-Razeel* divide. How funny and mischievous he was!

Hazrat Ayub Ansari belonged to Banu Najjar tribe of Yemen which earned global fame in the art of weaving. In those primitive days, Yaman was known world over for the production of finest class of fabrics. In India, the weavers of the Momin-Ansar community have long been known as highly skilled in the art of weaving. It is because of this basic fact that in India too, the community has always been identified as *'Bunker Biradri'* (weavers' caste) despite the fact that in India, the Ansari community has got the reputation of being good artisans also. In the states of Bihar, Uttar Pradesh, West Bengal, Orissa, Maharashtra, Delhi and Haryana, a large section of the community is engaged in handloom and powerloom industries, Ansaris have earned reputation as top class artisans also, mostly in Uttar Pradesh. They have equally excelled in wood carving of Saharanpur, carpet weaving in Bhadohi and Mirzapur, glass work of Ferozepore, artistic designing of Moradabadi utensils and Zari work for Benarsi Sarees. In Rajasthan, members of the community are engaged in diamond cutting and in lock industry, Aligarh. Significantly, all these artistic works find great admiration in countries outside India for which the country is earning huge foreign exchange. India is proud of these artisans.

Yemen to Medina

In ancient times, Yemen (Jordan) was one of the most developed and the richest country in the world. Jordan was famous for textile industry and agriculture and was industrially far ahead with the rest of the world. The unique 'Marab' dam for agriculture was then considered wonder of the world. Three miles in length and three miles in width, Marab stored water collected from seventy small rivulets. It was a rich source of irrigation that made Jordan the most advanced agricultural nation.

Going by the Islamic history, Qahtan bin Sa'am bin Nooh (Noah) was the forefather of the Yemen nation. The first king of Yemen was Saba bin Yashhab bin Ya'arasb bin Qahtan. He ruled for over four hundred eighty four years. His name was Abdus Shams and Saba was his title. After the King's name Saba became the name of the city and the nation. Historians describe him as a Muslim who believed in one God but the rest of nation prayed sun.

In the human history known so far, Saba was the most rich and highly cultured nation in the world. People used to dine in silver plates and had golden utensils. Sandal wood, coriander and other perfumed wood were used as fuel in households. The palaces and even houses were unique show pieces of architecture. Saba was the most beautiful town and the twenty storied majestic palace of Umda'n with one hundred rooms had each story 36 ft in height.

The unbounded wealth and the luxuries of life ultimately brought in all sorts of evil in the society, so much so, that they invited the wrath of the almighty. In the midst of the fifth century, the pride of Yemen, the Marab dam burst which flooded entire Saba. Due to unprecedented floods, the agricultural land became marshy and uncultivable. Moreover, the floods caused havoc to the entire nation. It was upside down for a nation which till the other day, was the richest in the world.

Historians have written that after the catastrophe of *'Saile Iram'* as is popularly known in Arab world, a number of tribes left Yemen and migrated to Egypt, Syria, Iraq and other countries. They settled on the banks of Firat. Imran bin Amir, who was the forefather of Ansars had left Yemen before Saile Iram, Sa'alba who was the nephew of Imran bin Amir, migrated to Yasrab (Madina). Haarsa was the son of Sa'alba who had two sons, Oas and Khazraj. Oas had only one son Malik bin Oas, while Khazraj had five. The descendants of Oas and Khazraj spread over in Medina where they settled. They were first to accept Islam. Hazrat Ayub Ansari was from khazraj generations.

After Prophet Mohammad attained Prophethood, he started propagating Islam. It was his usual practice that during Haj season, he used to reach out to each and every tribe and invite them to the fold of Islam. Once it so happened that he went to the place where

Ansars were staying. They were altogether six Hajis from Yemen. Prophet Mohammed approached them, recited holy Quran and invited them to Islam. They were so mesmerised by the divine words of Quran that they did not loose any time and embraced Islam. When they went back to Medina, they narrated the entire story and propagated Islam among the Oas and Khazraj tribes. This was very much welcomed by the Ansars who made a bee line to Mecca to meet the Prophet and embrace Islam. Prophet Mohammad sent Um Makhtoom and Moasir bin Umair to Medina to teach Quran to the Ansars. Before Prophet Mohammad migrated to Medina, entire Medina had accepted Islam.

Hazrat Md. Ayub Ansari

When Prophet Mohammad migrated (Hijrat) to Medina from Mecca, Hazrat Ayub Ansari got the rare honour to play host to the prophet. As Prophet Mohammad entered Medina on his camel's back, every Muslim of Medina had a desire to host his Prophet. It was difficult for the Prophet to select his host and declared that he will stay in the house where the camel finally ends the journey. And it was Ayub Ansari's house, in front of which the camel sat. Prophet Mohammad stayed for seven months in the house of Hazrat Ayub Ansari. It was this rare honour to host the prophet Mohammad that made Ayub Ansari, the most distinguished and highly respected amongst prophet's companions (Sahabas). Prophet Mohammad had his special fascination for cloth woven by the weavers of Abu Najjar tribe to which Hazrat Ayub Ansari belonged.

Name of Hazrat Ayub Ansari was Khalid alias Abu Ayub. After the death of Prophet Mohammad, Hazrat Ayub was greatly frustrated. He left his weaving work and set on for taking part in a number of religious battles. He was a great warrior. He made his first mark as a warrior against Egypt under the command of Umar-bin-Al'Aas. He showed his skill as a warrior under Hazrat Ali, who made him commander of the army. He was made Governor of Medina. During the reign of Hazrat Moaviah, he took part in the battle against Cyprus and in three attacks on Constantinpole. During the Constantinople war, epidemic broke out in Bazantine kingdom of Constantinople killing tens of thousands of persons. Hazrat Ayub lost his valuable life to the epidemic that struck Constantinople in 52 Hijri. He was buried under the Constantinople wall out of his will. Ayub Ansari died at the age of ninety.

Moaz bin Jabal Ansari

He was a weaver, also from Yemen. He was one of the most favourite companions of Prophet Mohammad for whom he once said that on the final Day of Judgment, Moaz will be the head of Ulemas. During the Khilafat of Banu Ummaiya, a number of Ansari families migrated to North India in the army of Mohammad bin Qasim. Sons of Sayyadul Ansar Hazrat Moaz bin Jabal Ansari also migrated to North India.

Mohallib bin Abi Safra Ansari

He had completed his tenure as the Governor of Khorasan, with an army of two hundred Ansaris, entered India through Khyber Pass in 45 Hijri and conquered Punjab. A large number of Ansaris were in the army of Mohammad bin Qausim Saqfi Ansari, who conquered Sindh. Abdullah Ansari was the son of Hazrat Ayub Ansari. During the reign of Caliph Hazrat Umar, while his father was still alive, he was appointed Governor of Hirat. He had two sons, Yusuf Ansari and Yaqub Ansari. Shibli Nomani wrote in 'Al-Mamoon' that these weaver families were both great warriors and courageous.

Islamic history, elaborated in depth, presents the theory that Ansaris in India were mostly the descendants of Yaqub Ansari and Yusuf Ansari, grand sons of Hazrat Ayub Ansari. They spread over the length and breadth of the country. Noted historian Shaikh Halim Sharar wrote that after the martyr of his father Abdullah Ansari, Yusuf Ansari alongwith his wife and children came to Sindh with Mohammad Bin Qasim where he died in 96 Hijri. He was a brave warrior and most of the victories of Mohammad Bin Qasim are attributed to Yusuf Ansari. After Mohammad Bin Qasim was dislodged from governorship by the new caliph of Damascus Sulaiman Abdul Malik, Yazid was appointed governor in place of Qasim who was imprisoned. Sons of Yusuf Ansari left Sindh and migrated to the North border from where the area of Jaisalmer begins. Warriors from the Ansari community including Abdur Rahman Ansari (the great grand son of Yusuf Ansari) bin Jalaluddin Ansari bin Abul Hassan Ansari and other great grand sons Qasim Ansari and Yunus Ansari sons of Md. Saleh Ansari were in the army of Amiruddin Subuktagin (died in 997) who defeated Raja Jaipal of Delhi in 979.

Abdur Rahman Ansari bin Jalaluddin Ansari bin Abul Hassan Ansari was the great grand son of Yusuf Ansari. Qasim Ansari and Yunus Ansari bin Mohammad Saleh Ansari were also great grand sons of Yusuf Ansari. Their generations settled in Sindh, Jaipur, Jaisalmer, Bikaner, Khirpur and other places in Rajputana and adjoining areas. It is historically established fact that Yaqub Ansari, son of Abdullah Ansari permanently settled in Hirat. Sufi-poet Shaikh Abdullah Ansari, the Pir of Hirat, was one of Yaqub Ansari's sons. His full name was Abu Ismael Abdullah Ansari. Mallik Mahmood Shah Anju Aaq Khawaja, who was appointed ruler of Persia during the Ghaznavi period, was a relative of Pir Ansari. Mansoor Al Ansari, who was popularly known as Maulana Mohammad Mian had unique contribution to the Reshmi Roomal movement of Shaikh Mahmoodul Hassan to his credit. His son, Abdul Hamid Ansari was a freedom fighter and a renowned Urdu journalist of Bombay. The founder of Arabic education centre in Farangi Mahal, Lucknow, Mulla Nizamuddin bin Mulla Qutbuddin Sahalvi Shaheed was also a descendant of Hazrat Ayub Ansari. Yahya bin Zakaria and Mansoor Ansari, sons of Yakub Ansari came to India along with Mahmood Ghaznavi during his sixth attack and settled in Punjab. Their generations spread over to Rawalpindi, Sialkot, Ludhiana, Gujranawala, Mt. Gomri, Jhang, Vazirabad, Casoor, Lahore, Jhelum, Firozepore, Jalandhar, Patiala, Amritsar, Layalpur, Gurdaspur.

Hazrat Momin Arif

During the reign of Shahabuddin Ghauri, a warrior and a preacher of Islam from Yemen, Momin Arif bin Abdur Rahman Ansari, bin Jalaluddin Ansari bin Abul Hassan Ansari came over to India, conquered Maner, situated twenty miles West of Patna on the confluence of Sone and Ganges, in 576 A.D. He was the great grand son of Abdur Rahman 'Shaheed Pahelwan' who was the grand son of Abul Hassan Ansari who came from the generation of Yusuf Ansari. He migrated to India with his entire family and settled permanently at Maner Sharif. Hazrat Momin Arif was the first Muslim to settle in Maner. Sufi Maneri has written about Hazrat Momin Arif that he was a saint who used to offer five time prayers in Baitullah, Mecca. People of the area were fed up with the tyrinical rule of Raja Manyer. Hazrat Momin Arif waged war against Raja Manyer. Prophet Mohammad directed Hazrat Taj Faqih in his dream (Basharat) to go to Maner and assist Momin Arif in his war against Raja Manyer. Ultimately Raja Manyer was defeated and he fled Maner Sharif ('Sufi Maneri-Hayat Aur Shaeri', Dr. Khalid Rashid Saba).

Professor Hafiz Shamsuddin 'Shams Maneri', who belonged to Manershrif, wrote a poem on 'Maner Sharif', a couple of lines are quoted here:

> *"Janab Momin Arif key noor-e-imaan Sai; Nigah-e-Shauq Mein Mumtaaz Hai Maner Sharif"*

Generation after generations of Momin Arif spread over to the states of Bihar, Bengal, and Orissa and could be traced as far as Dacca, now in Bangladesh. Momin Arif died at Maner and his grave lies on the western flank of Maner Dak Bungalow. Momin Arif's son was popularly known as Ghazi Mian. For a long period, every year *'Ghazi Mian ki Shaadi Ka Mela'* used to be held at Maner Sharif. (From the article of Abdur Rahim Jayasi- *'Najabat-o-Sharafat*)

In his book, *'Al-Minwaal-o-Ahla'*, Abdus Salam Mubarakpuri, giving reference to Abdul Halim Sharar and other historians, has written that the grand son of Hazrat Ayub Ansari, Hazrat Yusuf and Momin Arif came over to India from Arab and Middle East.

Abdur Rahman Ansari bin Jalaluddin Ansari bin Abul Hassan Ansari was Raeesul-Mohaddisin and a brave warrior. Their entire family alongwith other relations settled in a Mauza on the bank of river Atak. When Salar Ghazi Masood came over to the Mauza, Abdur Rahman Ansari who was a known wrestler joined the army of Ghazi Masood. In the way, Ghazi Masood deputed Abdur Rahman Ansari and Mir Imamuddin Khilji to encircle and conquer fort Udaya Nagar which was renamed Jayasi, (Maraat-Masoodi by Shaikh Abdur Rahman Chishti). Both were killed only after they had already conquered Jayasi.

Mohammad-bin-Abdullah Ansari was forefather of the Ansari community of Gujarat. There was thick population of Ansari community in Ahmedabad and Baroda, now, Vadodra. Their fore fathers came over to India along with the army of Mohammad bin Qasim in the province of Sindh from where they migrated to Gujarat. Ansari community of Gujarat like Memon Bohra community, used to go for Haj pilgrimage every year.

During the reign of Ghayasuddin Balban, Delhi had a thick population of the Ansari community and out of fifteen important Mohallas of Delhi, one had a large number of Momin-Ansar. Most of them were engaged in weaving profession. In search of new avenues of livelihood, they migrated to Meerut, Roorkie, Saharanpur and Panipat. Prince Mohammad Ansari, son of Ghayasuddin Balban was a great patron of religious education. He had high regards for those who were highly educated in Islamic Sharia. This fascinated a saint from Hirat, Khawja Mohammad Ali, one of the sons of Shaikhul Islam, Khawja Abdullah Ansari, came over to Panipat and settled there. The King admired Khawja Mohammad Ali and bestowed upon him important positions in his kingdom. Generations of Khawja Mohammad Ali formed the bulk of population of the Ansari community in Panipat. Handloom clothes woven by the Ansaris of Panipat were famous in the entire country.

Tamim Ansari

During the lifetime of Prophet Mohammad (peace be on him), Muslims from Arab came to India primarily as tradesmen and saints. Among them was one Tamim Ansari, a companion (Sahaba) of Hazrat Mohammad. He belonged to Banu Najar tribe. His full name was Tamim bin Zayad al Ansari. He was born in Medina and died in India. He was buried in Kovalam, Tamil Nadu by the Nawab of Arcot, Nawab Saadatullah Khan in around 180.

From all these historical accounts it is clear beyond any doubt that since the very lifetime of Prophet Mohammad, India became a favourite place for the Arabs, mostly the off springs of Hazrat Ayub Ansari came not only for trade promotion and propagation of Islam amongst the God fearing people of this country but also with the purpose to settle down for ever. Even mostly among those who came over to India as warriors with their masters got enchanted with the vast wealth resources of this country, its peaceful environment and above all, its people. While their masters went back with the looted wealth, they preferred not to go back to their original places.

Prophet Mohammad, it is generally believed, though not substantiated by any authentic Hadith, once told his Sahabaas (companions) that he felt cool breeze from the side of Al-Hind, meaning thereby that the people of that country were God fearing and very humanly (Syed Sulaiman Nadvi: *'Arab-Hind Ta'lluqaat'*).

Allama Dr. Iqbal gave poetic shape to this saying. He wrote,

> *"Meer-e- Arab Ko Aai Thandi Hawa Jahan Sai:*
> *Mera Watan Wahi Hai, Mera Watan Wahi Hai".*

Farangi Mahal Ansaris

There have been a lot of misgivings about the Momin Ansar community hailing from Farangi Mahal and also about the other non-weavers class of the Momin community. The fact of the matter is that they all belong to one and the same Momin community. Only a section of this community has been engaged in weaving which they inherited from their ancestors, but another large section of this community is highly educated and engaged in different professions. They held high positions in the government and in academic fields, judiciary, engineering and medical faculties and enjoyed honour and dignity in the social life of the Muslim community. But this fact has been ignored deliberately in some cases.

In Uttar Pradesh, the same is the case with Farangi Mahal Ansaris. There are Muslims who do not believe and will never accept the fact that Farangi Mahal Ansaris were also from the Momin-Ansar community. It is equally true that most of the Farangi Mahal Ansaris themselves considered being different from Momin-Ansar community for the sake of false honour and dignity in the society. They are well educated, ranging from Ulemas to doctors, engineers, professors, etc. They have put themselves in a different class. While most of them have even limited their marital relationship amongst the so-called upper caste Muslims in the past, I found that a section of them have marital relations of their sons and daughters with other sections of Momin-Ansar families. In short, the Farangi Mahal Ansaris, though identified of a different class, because of their education and distinct culture, are no different and very much of the Momin-Ansar community.

During my long stay at Delhi in the mid seventies in connection with the 10th national session of the All India Momin Conference,

I had the opportunity to meet and interact with a host of Farangi Mahal Ansaris, on different occasions. I was very keen to know the basis of the general belief, which I understand was very much made out by interested quarters of within Farangi Mahal and outside, that the Farangi Mahal Ansaris were different from Momin-Ansar community. One of the persons I met was Md. Yasin Ansari. He was from an illustrious family but he did not keep secret of the fact that he was very much from Momin-Ansar community. He was the Principal of Aligarh Muslim University Engineering College. He was the son-in-law of prominent personality of the Momin community from Lucknow, Zafrul Hassan, Advocate. His eldest son Dr. Masood Azhar serving in Kuwait; another son, Mashood Ashhar, reader in civil engineering in Aligarh; younger two sons Belal and Sulaiman are also engineers while only daughter, Yasmin, is a doctorate in zoology. Yasin Ansari, during our conversations, unfolded upon me the truth about the Farangi Mahal Ansaris. He told me that the Farangi Mahal Ansaris or other educated class of Ansaris who have held positions at government or public levels and who command great respect in the society are very much scared of the stigma of being called '*Julaha*' and looked down upon in the society. They feared to be drawn in inferiority complex. This made others to make out that they were not Ansaris but of a different class because they were not weavers and had no marital relationship with the momin community as well. This is the main reason why they always kept themselves aloof from Momin community, more precisely the weaver's community. He asserted that very few amongst us are bold enough to publicly accept that yes, we are from the traditional Momin-Ansar community. Md. Yasin Ansari had enlightened me on this controversial issue which gets further strengthened with the interview of the veteran Congress leader Dr. Mukhtar Ahmad Ansari by Prof. Mujeeb and my confrontation with Sultana Hayat wife of Hayatullah Ansari on the subject (as stated earlier).

History of Farangi Mahal

In Lucknow, around four hundred years ago, there lived a French businessman named Nael. The Farangi Mahal belonged to Nael. He abandoned his business in India and left the country. The government confiscated his property. During the reign of Aurangzeb, the king gifted the Farangi Mahal to his religious adviser Mulla Asad bin Qutubuddin Sahlvi Shaheed and his brother, descendants of Hazrat Ayub Ansari. They developed Farangi Mahal into a full fledged Islamic School with modern teachings. Very soon, Farangi Mahal came to be known as a centre of excellence for Islamic studies. It was often compared to Oxford and Cambridge. However, presently it has lost its sheen.

Qutbuddin Shaheed Sahalvi and Mulla Nizamuddin, who authored *Darse Nizami* taught in Islamic institutions, were offsprings of Ayub Ansari and the products of Farangi Mahal. Other notables from Farangi Mahal included Waliul Haque Ansari, former HOD, Persian Department, Lucknow University; Professor Anwer Ansari, Department of Psychology, A.M.U.; Dr. Ghaus Ansari who did his doctorate from Australia University and wrote a book '*U.P. Mein Muslim Jatiyaan*'; Asloob Ahmad Ansari, Department of English, A.M.U.; Mehdi Ansari, Department of Arabic, A.M.U.; and Iqbal Ansari, a renowned author who is no more. With high education which envisaged rich culture, they occupied responsible positions in the society. It was but natural, that they have been distinctly different: socially and culturally, from those engaged in weaving and other professions. Despite the fact that large number of the Ansar community engaged in weaving profession in Benaras, carpet weaving in Bhadohi, silk weaving in Bhagalpur, brass and wood carving and other industries were financially more sound than most of the Farangi Mahal Ansaris, it is interesting to note that while the weavers and artisans were looked down upon, humiliated and subjugated by the so-called upper caste Muslims because of their educational and social superiority, the Farangi Mahal Ansaris were classified differently and were considered class apart. In most cases, they do not mind marrying their children to those of Farangi Mahal Ansaris. In the background of the historical facts, it seems that the myth woven around the Farangi Mahal Ansaris was wrong. However, there are such responsible persons even today, suffering from class-phobia that they are always ready to sharply react if any Ansari who has attained high position in public life if rightly claimed as a person from the Momin-Ansar community.

Ansari Luminaries

Dr. Mokhtar Ahmad Ansari

One of the topmost luminaries from the Ansari community was

Dr. Mokhtar Ahmad Ansari. About him also, it was made to believe that Dr. Ansari was also a Farangi Mahal Ansari and not from the traditional Momin-Ansar community. Prof. Mashirul Hassan authored a book on Dr. Mukhtar Ahmad Ansari, published by the Publication Division, Information & Broadcasting, Government of India. In this publication, Mashirul Hassan has given reference to Prof. Md. Mujeeb's interview of Dr. Ansari. Dr. Mukhtar Ahmad Ansari was the towering personality of the Congress party of that period but was shamelessly ignored by the Congress party and its government.

Professor Mashirul Hassan writes "Dr. Ansari's family claimed it's ancestry with Ayub Ansari, but they never liked to be equated or linked with the weaver's community as the weavers in India were looked down upon even by a section of the community itself and were identified with derogatory word *'Julaha'*. Since they also claim to be from the generations of Ayub Ansari. Dr. Mukhtar Ahmad Ansari had a quiet but deep pride in his ancestry. It pleased him to think that his roots lay deep into the soil of Arabia and he belonged to a distinguished family with branches spread over different parts of the country. Professor Mohammad Mujeeb, then a teacher of the Jamia Millia Islamia records an interview in which he quotes Dr. Ansari as saying, "My family originates from Ansaris. But then he stopped, and laughed. Why should one imagine that Ansaris are few? There are as many as destined to be."

Khawja Hamiduddin, who was from the generations of Ayub Ansari, had migrated to Shiraz with his three sons. His sons later moved to Delhi. One of his sons was appointed a Qauzi by Mohammad Bin Tughlaque. His nephew continued with the job of Qauzi after his death. This nephew was the founder of the village Yusufpore in Ghazipore where Dr. Ansari was born. His father Abdur Rahman Ansari, a descendant of Hazrat Ayub Ansari was Sadar Ameen of Balia district at Rasara under Company's government. During the first war of independence in 1857, he opted in support to the British government. In recognition to the loyal services he rendered to the British in the 1857 revolt, he received a small estate near Yusufpore. He was also granted exemption from Arms Act. But all his three sons, Hakim Abdul Wahab Ansari with handicapped vision, Hakim Abdur Razzaque Ansari, and the youngest Dr. Mokhtar Ahmad Ansari were deeply associated with India's independence movement.

Dr. Mokhtar Ahmad Ansari was born on December 25, 1880 and expired on May 10, 1936. Dr. Ansari got his early education from Victoria High School. He did his Intermediate from Muir Central College, Allahabad in 1896. His family moved to Hyderabad where he graduated from Nizam College. Later, he went to England on scholarship studies and achieved M.D. and M.S. degrees. He was at the age of twenty one that he sailed for London. He spent a couple of weeks in accommodation provided for new arrivals. Then he left for Edinbugh to join the Medical College. There he secured the degree of Doctor of Medicine and Master of Surgery in 1908. An Indian pioneer in surgery, Dr. Ansari worked at London Lock Hospital and Charing Cross Hospital. There is an Ansari ward in Charing Cross Hospital in his honour.

During war of Bilqaan in the year 1912, by the efforts of Maulana Mohammad Ali, a medical team headed by Dr. Mokhtar Ahmad Ansari was sent to help the Turks. The Indian delegation, sent entirely on the expense of Indian Muslims included Shoaib Quraishi, Minister, Bhopal; Chowdhry Khaliquzzaman, Lucknow; Abdur Rahman Siddiqui, Bengal; and Abdul Aziz Ansari. Dr. Syed Abdur Rahman and Dr. Naeem Ansari, who had just finished their medical education, went straight to Constantinpole from London to join the medical mission.

After his safe return from the war front, Dr. Mokhtar Ahmad Ansari started taking active part in political activities. He joined Indian National Congress and Muslim League, both non-political organisations then. He played an important role in the negotiations of 1916 Lucknow Pact. He was an outspoken supporter of Khilafat movement and worked to bring Congress, Muslim League and Khilafat together on the issue against Mustafa Kamal's decision to oust the Sultan of Turkey and to protest recognition of Turky by the British Empire. He left Muslim League for its separatist policy.

Dr. Ansari was married to Shamsunnisa who died in 1938. She was a pliant wife and a good housekeeper. Visitor to Dr. Ansari's house as Khalida Edib, the Turkish author, remembered her as 'very pious and charitable'. She was associated with Anjuman-e-Khuddam-i-Kaaba.

With Dr. Mukhtar Ahmad Ansari, the family emerged from the position of old Ghazipur family into national prominence. His close relatives, Aziz Ansari, Faridul Haque Ansari and Shaukutullah Ansari played important roles in national politics.

Aziz Ansari joined the Indian Medical Mission to Constantinpole and went to jail during both the non-cooperation movement and civil disobedience agitation. Faridul Haque Ansari was member of All India Congress Committee (AICC) from 1927 to 1949, Secretary of Delhi Pradesh Congress Committee from 1929-30. Shaukatullah Ansari, a nephew of Dr. Ansari who was married to his adopted daughter Zohra, floated various organisations in support of Congress in the mid of 1940, notables being Azad Muslim Board and All India Muslim Majlis.

Dr. Ansari was very close to Mahatma Gandhi. He was a staunch nationalist and patriot. He was for several terms General Secretary of the Indian National Congress and its president in the year 1927. His palatial house, 'Darus Salam' in Delhi's Darya Gunj was the centre of political activities. The road where the house was situated has been named Ansari Road. Those days in Delhi, Darus Salam attained the same importance as Anand Bhawan at Allahabad. All the top leaders of the Congress party in its early period of political movement used to converge in Darya Gunj. Along with Dr. Zakir Hussain, Ajmal Khan and Hussain Ahmad Madni, Mokhtar Ahmad Ansari was the founder of Jamia Millia Islamia. He became its Chancellor in 1927 after the death of Hakim Ajmal Khan.

Dr. Mohammad Hamid Ansari

Another most distinguished person in the Ansari community is Hamid Ansari. The 14th Vice-President of Indian Republic, Hamid Ansari, the son of Mohammad Abdul Aziz Ansari comes from a renowned nationalist family. He comes from Ghazipur and is grand nephew of Dr. Mukhtar Ahmad Ansari. Dr. Hamid Ansari became the only person after S. Radhakrishnan to get a second term as the Vice-President.

Dr. Hamid Ansari is a thorough gentleman, soft spoken and impeccably mannered. With an array of impressive assignments all over the globe as a diplomat in a career spanning about fifty years. He is highly educated. After obtaining Master in Political Science, he got double doctorate from Simla's Str. Edward School and Calcutta's St Xavier's College.

In the course of compilation of this book, I had the honour of meeting the Vice-President of Indian Republic, Hamid Ansari who clarified his relationship with Dr. Mokhtar Ahmad Ansari. He told me that Dr. Mukhtar Ahmad Ansari was maternal uncle (*mamoon)* of his father? On another occasion, a few months before he became the Vice-President, Hamid Ansari came to Patna to deliver his speech on, '*Khilafat Aur Uski Ahmiat*" in the Khuda Bakhsh Oriental Public Library. After the function was over, during the course of his informal chat with invitees present there, he clearly spoke about his connection with Dr. Mokhtar Ahmad Ansari.

He was born in Calcutta on April 1, 1937. He is an academician, a career diplomat and a former Vice-Chancellor of Aligarh Muslim University from 2000 to 2002. He was awarded 'Padma Shree' in 1984. He started his career as a civil servant in the Indian Foreign Service in 1961. He was a permanent representative of India to the United Nations, Indian High Commissioner to Australia and Ambassador to the United Arab Emirates, Afghanistan, Iran and Saudi Arabia. He also served as Chairman, National Minority Commission from 2006 to 2007.

Hayatullah Ansari

One out of the Farangi Mahal Ansaris was Hayatullah Ansari. He was a staunch congressman, prominent literary figure, journalist, a novelist and Urdu scholar. He was a recipient of Sahitya Academy Award in 1970 for his Urdu novel, '*Lahoo-Ke-Phool*' written in 1949 in five volumes. He wrote another novel '*Ghironda*' in the year 1982. His wife Sultana Hayat was equally a scholar of Urdu language of high repute. Hayatulla Ansari was the Editor of 'Qaumi Awaz', Urdu edition of *National Herald* brought out by Jawahar Lal Nehru. After retirement from '*Qaumi Awaaz*', he was nominated to the Rajya Sabha. He was also made in charge of the Congress party's organ, '*Sub-Saath*' in Urdu at its headquarters in Delhi. He was a staunch nationalist and a pillar of secular ideals. Hayatullah Ansari was highly respected by the leadership of the party.

In the year 1972, the editors of the Urdu newspapers of Bihar organized and established All India Urdu Editor's Conference with its head quarters at Patna. Urdu editors from all over the country, including Hayatullah Ansari attended the founding session, presided over by Kuldip Nayyar. Hayatullah Ansari was then the Editor of '*Qaumi Awaaz*', Lucknow. He was chosen unanimously the first president of the editor's body.

My personal relation with Hayatullah Ansari and his wife Sultana Hayat grew thereafter. In the years afterwards during most of their visit to Patna, I had the opportunity to host them on a couple of occasions.

I had shifted to Delhi to make preparations for the historic 10th session of the All India Momin Conference. The then Prime Minister Smt. Indira Gandhi had allotted a bungalow from the Rajya Sabha pool, 14 C Firozeshah Road for the office of the All India Momin Conference. I was then the Secretary of the All India Momin Conference and also in charge of the central office at Delhi. Those days, Hayatullah Ansari was editing Congress organ '*Sub-Saath*'. I used to meet him often. Once it so happened that Sultana Hayat was also present there, she requested me to drop her in the way. While we were on our way, Sultana questioned me why Ziaur Rahman Ansari did not accommodate Hayatullah in the working committee of the All India Momin Conference. Ziaur Rahman Ansari was the Union Minister and President of the All India Momin Conference. I was surprised over her outburst on the subject as never before they took any interest in the organization rather kept themselves aloof from all activities of the Momin Conference. Moreover, Hayatullah Ansari never claimed earlier to be from the Momin community and kept others guessing about his caste credentials. However, her self revealing came as a pleasant surprise to all of us.

Altaf Hussain Hali

The great Urdu poet Khawja Altaf Hussain Hali was born in Panipat in the year 1253 A.H. His father was from Ansari community and mother was a Syed from Shohdapur.

Altaf Hussain Hali in the preface of his famed book, '*Musaddas Hali*' writes that in Panipat there is a big Mohalla named Ansarian inhabited by the Momin-Ansar community where he lived. He wrote that his father was from Momin-Ansar community while mother was a Syed.

(The author had the opportunity to go to Panipat in the year 1976. He was delighted to see the well laid beautiful park named after him in his memory by the side of the express way between Delhi and Panipat. Bashir Ansari, an activist of the Momin Conference took him to Mohallah Ansarian in Panipat to offer Fateha at the Mazar of Altaf Hussain Hali.)

Khawja Ahmad Abbas

He was born in Panipat in the house of Altaf Hussain Hali. Hali was his great grandfather. Abbas took his early education from Hali Muslim High School. Khawja Ahmad Abbas had a very glorious record of life. He was a novelist, journalist and film director. His column 'last page' in the weekly "Blitz" (Hindi, Urdu and English) holds the distinction of being the longest running column in the history of Indian journalism which continued till his death in 1987. He was awarded Padma Shri in 1969. His family tree goes back to Hazrat Ayub Ansari.

M.J. Akbar

Mobashir Javed Akbar, a veteran Indian journalist and author comes from a Momin-Ansar community. Son of Md. Akbar, was born on January 11, 1951. He got his early education in Telnipara, town of jute mills in Hoogly district of West Bengal. Later, he moved to Calcutta from where he graduated. Akbar married Mallika Joseph and has two children, Parayag and Mukulika.

Youngest of the three, Mobashir's elder sister was married to Md. Halim Ansari who retired as an officer of Reserve Bank of India. He died recently at Patna. His daughter is married to Samiullah Ansari, a practicing lawyer of Patna High Court. He hails from Jhajha now in Jharkhand. Samiullah is the son of Md. Ibrahim Ansari of Swadeshi Biri Companywho during the early days of the movement played a very significant role. The younger sister was married to Saghir Ansari. He did Commerce and law from Patna University. He started his career as a teacher in Calcutta and later shifted to practicing law. Presenty, he lives in Delhi.

As told by late Abdur Rauf Ansari, former West Bengal Minister and a prominent Momin leader of Bengal, Mr. Akbar, his father was closely associated with the Momin Movement in its early days.

Mobashir Javed started his journalistic career in 1971 from *Times of India*. He was so brilliant that only within a short period, he made his presence felt in the world of print media. He jumped over the ladders of success of his journalistic career. In 1982, after the success of *Sunday*, Akbar launched the first modern newspaper, '*The Telegraph*' from Calcutta. He was known for his balanced and fearless writings on the conspiracy behind the communal riots that had overtaken the nation. He launched '*The Sunday Gaurdian*, a weekly newspaper in 2010'. He is the founder and former Editor-in-Chief and Managing Director of "*The Asian Age*".

Mobashir Javed authored books *"The Shade of Swords"*, *"Riot after Riot in India"*, *"Nehru, The Making of India"*, *"The Seige Within"* besides others.

After coming in prominence, he was picked up by the Congress party. He became a member of parliament from Muslim dominated Kishanganj. A prominent Muslim face in the Congress party, Prime Minister Rajiv Gandhi made him his official spokesman. He was nominated by the Union government in a number of important government agencies. However, he lost the confidence of Kishanganj voters that made him loose the membership of Lok Sabha in the next elections. He again turned to journalism in 1982. Presently, Akbar has joined Bharatiya Janata Party (BJP).

Khalid Ansari

His full name is Khalid Abdul Hamid Ansari. He is the illustrious son of Abdul Hamid Ansari, a nationalist and a Congressman. He was the founder of Inquilab Publications Ltd. in 1937 which published *"Inquilab"* Urdu daily from Bombay during freedom movement. He was awarded Padma Shri in 2001.

Khalid Ansari is a journalist of repute. Right in the footsteps of his father, he founded Mid-Day group of Publications and became its chairman alongwith that of Inquilab Publications. *Mid-day* became the best selling weekly of the country. Khalid Ansari made his presence felt in the cricket world. He wrote a number of books on cricket. Presently, Khalid Ansari is assigned as Safety Advisor and Training officer at Teekay Offshore Dams, Australia.

Prominent Ansaris in other Countries

Pakistan: Ansaris are mostly settled in Karachi and Hyderabad. They have lost their caste identity and have fully mingled with Urdu speaking Muhajirs.

Zafar Ishaque Ansari, born 27 December 1932 is a scholar of Islamic Studies. He is the Director General of the Islamic Research Institute of the International Islamic University. Previously, he has also been the President of the International Islamic University Islamabad. He has published a number of books and articles, and has spoken at international conferences on Islamic Studies and inter-religious dialogues. Zafar Ishaq Ansari belongs to a family of scholars. His late father Maulana Zafar Ahmed Ansari was also a renowned and respectable scholar of Islamic Studies and was also elected to the National Assembly of Pakistan during the 1970s. Dr. Ansari obtained his M.A. and PhD from the Institute of Islamic Studies, McGill University, Montreal, Canada in 1966. His main thesis for his PhD program was titled "The Early Development of Fiqh in Kufah with special reference to the works of Abu Yusuf and Shaybanm". He studied at University of Karachi before going to Canada for his higher studies. He was also associated with *Islami Jamiat-e-Talaba*.

Dr. Ansari has a flair for languages as well. While he is proficient and fluent in English, Urdu (his native language) and Arabic, he has a good command over Persian, French and German as well.

Md. Hanif Ansari and Md. Akram Ansari, both members of the national assembly in Pakistan; and Md. Tajuddin Ansari is a prominent politician.

Saudi Arabia: Abdur Rahman Ansari, Professor of Archeology, King Saud University, member, 1st and 2nd terms of Consultative Assembly, Saudi Arabia.

Nepal: Salim Miyan Ansari is a senior politician of Nepal, was Minister for forests and soil conservation. He was once a minister for tourism also; Dr. Zainuddin Ansari is Chairman of National Medical College, Birgunj, Nepal.

Egypt: Zakariyya al-Ansari, Egyptian Sufi mystic, an Islamic scholar.

U.K.: Khizer Hayat Ansari is a British academic who was awarded OBE in 2002 for his work on ethnic and racial relations. He has migrated from Lahore. His son Zafar Ansari is a known Surrey country cricketer.

U.S.A.: Aziz Ansari, a famed small screen American comedian/ Actor, is the son of Shaukath Ansari, a gastro-entrologist and Fathima. They migrated from Chennai, India. Born on 23 February, 1983 and graduated from New York University.

Azher Usman is the son of Zia Usman and Atia Usman who migrated to USA from Bihar, India and are based at Chicago. Attorney by profession, Azher Usman is America's most sought after comedian. He has been visiting different parts of the world with his troupe on invitation and is always under pressure. Azher Usman is the star attraction of the annual ISNA conferences.

Female Ansari Personalities

Anoushed Ansari, first female astronaut from Iran, made her mark in history. She has won the National Space Pioneer award held at a function in Toronto on April, 2015.

Suzana Ansari is English singer of Bangladeshi decent; and Bushra Ansari is Pakistan T.V. presentor, singer actress and comedian.

Galaxy of Islamic Scholars

The Momin-Ansar community is also proud of the fact that there has been a long list of Muftis, Ulemas and Mashaekhs to its fold who have held high positions in religious bodies of the country.

Rashid Ahmad Gongohi, a descendant of Hazrat Ayub Ansari, was an Indian Deobandi Islamic scholar, a leading figure of the Deobandi movement, a Hanafi jurist and scholar of hadith. Along with Muhammad Qasim Nanautawi, he was a pupil of Mamluk Ali. Both studied the books of hadith under Shah Abdul Ghani and later became Sufi disciples of Haji Imdadullah. His lectures on*Sahih al-Bukhari* and *Jami' at-Tirmidhi* were recorded by his student Muhammad Yahya Kandhlawi, later edited, arranged, and commented on by Muhammad Zakariya Kandhlawi, and published as *Lami' ad-Darari 'ala Jami' al-Bukhari* and *al-Kawkab ad-Durri 'ala Jami' at-Tirmidhi*. Rashid Ahmad was born on Monday, 6 Dhu al-Qi'dah 1244 AH (11 May 1829) in Gangoh, Saharanpur District, British India (in present-day Uttar Pradesh, India). He was born in the mohallah of Sarai. Both his father Maulana Hidayat Ahmad and his mother Karimun Nisa belonged to Ansari Ayyubi families, claiming descent from Abu Ayyub al-Ansari. His ancestral village was Rampur, but his grandfather Qazi Pir Bakhsh had settled in Gangoh. In 1297 AH, after the death of Qasim, Rashid was made *sarparast* (patron) of Darul Uloom Deoband. From 1314 AH he was also *sarparast* of the Darul Uloom's sister madrasah, Mazahir Uloom Saharanpur. He died on Friday, 8 Jumada II 1323 AH (11 August 1905) He authored 14 books on *fiqah* and *Sufism* including *Fatwa-e-Rashidya*.

Maulana Abdul Haque Ansari, Born on September 1, 1931 and died on October 3, 2012. Dr. Ansari was an Islamic scholar. He got degree in Arabic, Master and Doctorate from Aligarh Muslim University and pursued higher education in Comparative religion from Harvard University. Maulana Abdul Haque Ansari was *Amir Jamaet-e-Islami Hind* from 2003 to 2007. He was the Professor and Head of Department Arabic, Persian and Islamic Studies at Vishwa Bharti University. Maulana Mukhtar Ahmad Nadvi, was the Amir Jamaet Ahle-e-Hadis at national level. Maulana Arshadul Qaudri was the founder and Amir of Edara Shariah, with headquarters in Bihar. Maulana Abdul Wahab Arvi was vice-president of Jamiat Ulema Hind till his death and Maulana Fozail Ahmad headed the Markazi Jamiat Ulema with headquarters at Mehdian, New Delhi. Maulana Habibur Rahman Azmi, Maulana Abdullah Ghazipuri and Maulana Abdul Hameed Rahmani were great Islamic Scholars. Maulana Abdul Hamid Rahmani was born at a place known as Tendua Bazar in eastern U.P. He died in August last year.

Maulana Imamuddin Ramnagri: Banaras is situated on the western bank and just on opposite side is Ramnagar, a small township on the eastern bank of the river Ganges. Maulana hailed from Ramnagar. He came from a very poor family. His father was a tailor and he learnt tailoring from his father. He was a regular reader of Holy Quran. Whenever he got time; he would take the opportunity to recite few pages from Quran. Ramnagar had no facility for madarsa education. Incidentally, there was a Muslim Saees for the stable of Raja's horses. He was interested in teaching Muslim children. He started providing religious teachings in a small way. There were a number of pucca platforms provided for feeding the horses. A few boys of Ramnagar interested in Maktab education gathered around the Saees, their Maulvi Saheb. Imamuddin was one amongst them. Maulana got the basic madarsa education from the improvised Maktab. While one pucca platform was the make-shift Maktab, another platform served as a prayer place.

Maulana learnt primary Arabic from Hakim Naimuddin Saheb who was from Sasaram. He became Hafiz in a short period. He was so intelligent and brilliant that he gained deep knowledge of Quran. His educational knowledge was amazing. While he did not attend any regular Maktab, school or college, he acquired the vast knowledge of Urdu, Persian, Arabic and Sanskrit. He was a

Hafiz, a poet, a researcher, orator and what not and everything was god gifted. Maulana Imamuddin Ramnagri took keen interest in the Momin movement from early days. He attended the 10th session of the All India Momin Conference at Delhi under the presidentship of Ziaur Rahman Ansari. He died at the age of ninety.

Outstanding Personalities

Momin-Ansar community of India being 65 per cent of the entire Muslim population are spread over every part of the country. They are in administration, education and judiciary, politics, medicine, engineering, journalism and sports. Their presence is deeply felt in all spheres.

Presently in Bihar, Dy. Chairman of the Bihar Legislative Council is Md. Salim Pervez. He comes from Siwan and is a JD(U) leader. In U.P., Ahmad Hassan (SSP) is a senior minister of Akhilesh state government. In Parliament, Ali Anwar Ansari, JD(U) from Bihar and Salim Ansari (BSP) from U.P. are members of Council of States (Rajya Sabha). In the present cabinet of JD(U), Javed Ansari is the Minister for Tourism.

Notable in the field of judiciary, Justice Md. Iqbal Ansari is the senior most judge of Patna High Court, placed next to the Chief Justice. Before his transfer to Patna High Court from Guwahati, he had given his opinion about CBI's constitutional status that created furore in the corridors of power: Justice Md. Shamim, son-in-law of Md. Qadeer Ansari of Moradabad, was Metropolitan magistrate in Delhi when he heard the case of Indira Gandhi for her alleged acts of excesses during emergency. Later he rose to the bench of Delhi High Court. Justice Shamim was Lok Ayukt and Chairman of Central Minority Commission too. Anis Ansari was an I.A.S. officer serving in Uttar Pradesh. Presently, he is the Vice-Chancellor of Urdu, Arabic and Persian University in Lucknow.

Captain Haroon Anwar Arfi (younger brother of the author) was an I.A.S. officer serving in Delhi administration. He joined Indian army as 2nd Lt. in 1963 after competing successfully in emergency commission. During war with Pakistan in 1965, he was posted at the Chumb-Jurian sector.

Arfi successfully appeared at the I.A.S. exams in 1966. He was on deputation to the External Affairs Ministry and posted as First Secretary in the Indian High Commission, Kuwait. Before coming back to Delhi, he served as secretary to governor of Arunachal Pradesh.

Presently, there is an exhaustive list of I.A.S and I.P.S officers and those in the judiciary belonging to the Momin community serving in Bengal, Jharkhand, Bihar, U.P., M.P. and other states. To name a few, they are—M.W. Ansari, IPS, DG/Dir, Raipur; Asif Jalal, IPS, SP, CBI (Hqr), New Delhi; and Md. Abdur Rahman, IPS, Addl. Police Commissioner, Pune.

Besides, there are innumerable persons from the community in judicial and civil services of the states. Their number was still unsatisfactory considering its huge population. This was mainly because of lesser education opportunities for which number of factors worked. Even though this large section of the Momin-Ansar community had nothing to do with weaving, not even their forefathers ever took to weaving; others still prefer to identify them as from '*bunker biradri*' or '*Julaha*'. This way such people only derive satisfaction to their false ego.

The prime objective of compiling this book is to provide knowledge to both our present and future generations about this great movement that scripted history and for understanding our roots, ancestors and historic events. The chapter on Arab ancestry will enable interested readers, through eyes of imagination, to traverse deserts from Yemen to Medina, sail to Qustuntunia {Istanbole}, climb mountains on way to Hirat, swim rivers and finally march to reach India. Besides India, they travelled to Iran, Middle East, Afghanistan, Pakistan and Nepal Terai.

Momin Movement

Momin movement occupies the top of the notable nationalist movements that took birth in the state of Bihar and later, blossomed to shape the destiny of the nation. It created history when one single caste amongst the Muslim community of India, popularly known as the Momin community or the Ansaris, under its banner, found a place of honour and pride in the anals of Indian history in recognition of its unparallel role in the national struggle for freedom from British colonial rule. During the freedom movement, Momin Conference was the main mass organization of Muslims that stood firmly against the divisive forces of Muslim communalism. The repudiation of M.A. Jinnah's claim that Muslim League was the sole representative body of Indian Muslim by the vast Momin community found its echo in the House of Commons when two of its members, R.W. Sorensen and Silverman conveyed to L.S. Amery, Secretary of State for India on March 12, 1942, that a very large section of Indian Muslims were against Muslim League and were opposed to the division of the country on communal lines. The Momin community was of staunch nationalist outlook and was entirely with the Indian National Congress.

(To meet the challenges of communal politics, the Momin community took historic decision at the Gorakhpur session of Momin Conference in the year 1939, a social organisation till now, to convert it into a political entity. Ten years after, at the Patna session, it once again decided to reconvert it to a social body. The leadership, in good faith, issued appeal to the community to henceforth, join Congress, a party with strong secular credentials, in the hope that the party out of honest magnanimity take care of the educational, economic and political aspirations of the Momin community. The answer whether the Congress party could show its magnanimity and honesty in governance in regards to the community, could be found in the history of the last seventy years).

It is a story of a community or caste of India which has been for centuries a victim of subjugation and humiliation for their only fault that they were basically from occupational class, noble and extremely religious. In the feudal system that was prevalent in the country till independence, the Nawabs and Zamindars who had scant regard for religious teachings and humanity, exploited this group for their own benefits. These feudal lords found free labour in them, compelled them to work in their fields and personal establishments and used their influence to deny them any access to education.

Tracing the history, the story of misfortune of the Momin community takes us back to the days when the British set their feet on Indian soil for expanding trade in the grab of East India Company. Moreover, it had greater stake in India beyond trade. During that period, India had a very flourishing textile industry. Historians have recorded that there were a number of textile barons from the Momin community whose individual assets were something around that of the East India Company. The famous Dhaka Muslin produced by the Indian weavers on handlooms had no parallel in the global textile market. Even cloths produced by modern Manchester textile mills of UK could not measure up to the skill of the Indian weavers. The flourishing Indian textile industry and the wealth that was accumulated in India became the cynosure of the British eyes. The 'Dacca Muslin' was the classic fabric produced by Indian weavers, unmatched in the world. History is full of heart rending atrocities of the British rulers on the Indian weavers. After setting foot on the Indian soil, British made the weavers first target of their brutalities. The horror of cutting of thumbs and fingers of the weavers were carried out with the sole intention to destroy India's textile industry and push textiles manufactured in UK in India. This was a great blow to the Indian textile industry and economic setback for the weaver's community.

The Momin community or the Ansaris were already the victims of social disparities and caste system in the Muslim society. After the British landed in India, they lost their economic soundness also. Basically, it was barbarism and terror that let loose on the weavers by the East India Company which created a deep sense of hatred and revenge in the hearts and minds of the weaver's community against the British. Since early last century, consciousness started to grow in the Momin-Ansar community against their humiliating lives and the smuggled in caste system in the Indian Muslims. Their lives had become miserable. They were so much subjugated that they were not even allowed to live a peaceful and honourable life. Suffering from inferiority complex, they were scared to come openly against the un-Islamic behaviour of a section of the affluent class of the community.

Both these two factors lead to a spirited desire in the community to get rid of the British rule and help to bring in Swarajya in the country, on one hand. No less, there existed a strong urge in the community to fight out the social evil of caste system, and to bring about equality in the Muslim society, as per the sayings and spirit of Holy Quran and Hadith. The Ansaris expressed their determination to come out from the humiliating social life they were forced to live and to stand firmly against any act of oppression and subjugation by fellow Muslim brethren based entirely on false notions. History bears out the fact that the firm resolves of the Ansaris to rise against the twin evils of slavery and caste prejudices started showing signs from early days of Khilafat movement. Since those days, caste superiors were in such aggressive mood against those of the occupational beradris that it was beyond imagination for Muslims of the backward groups to gather moral strength to raise their voice against un-Islamic behaviour of high and mighty section of Muslim community. At the initial stage, in absence of any such organized movement, the members of the Momin-Ansar community, started whispering campaign mostly in the states of Uttar Pradesh, Delhi, Bihar and Bengal to create consciousness and to mobilize public opinion. They also started secret meetings in small groups to avoid any friction and undue reaction from the other side. This is how the historic movement came into existence.

Since early days when Calcutta was the capital of India, there was an exodus of people mostly from adjoining Bihar and United Provinces, in quest of vast opportunities for a better livelihood. They went there for higher studies, employments, for setting up business concerns, to work as labourers in factories and docks. Mostly these non-Bengali migrants found Calcutta a congenial place to live in. They settled and became an integral part of Calcutta's civic life. The Bengali population had never any problem with these Bihari settlers. Both mingled with each other maintaining their distinct language and culture. The non-Bengalis of Calcutta were called Calcatians. These settlers from Bihar and Uttar Pradesh were mostly from occupational biradris and more so from Momin-Ansar community.

I knew number of persons of the Momin-Ansar community who were leading traders. They belonged mostly to Bihar. Two most popular restaurants that were favourite for Calcatians were Amjadia and Aminia, being run by Ansaris. Amjadia was in Kolutola area, which faded away but Aminia in the New Market area, still continues to be the most favourite of the restaurants. Haji Abdul Qaiyum was the proprietor of Aminia Hotel with whom I had close acquaintance. He was a great admirer of all those who were spearheading the Momin movement and fully supported the move. After his death his sons are managing Aminia Hotel affairs. Amongst Ansari businessmen, Yatim Mia from Chakia, Champaran, Bihar had set up barrel business which was later looked after by his son, Farzand Ali. Haji Shamsuddin was one of the biggest name in paint business and Master Qausim of Gaya was a baron of Hawai chappal trade in the Topsia area of East Calcutta. Almost the entire vegetable business in the S.S. Hogg Vegetable market, situated next to New Market, which catered the need of bigger part of the city, was controlled by Ansaris. Three of the top businessmen in the vegetable trade, Md. Rafi, Md. Tabarak Hussain and Abdul Hamid were all from a village Rasulepore Katesar, two kilometers South of Manersharif in the district of Patna. Apart from business class, Ansaris could be found in other spheres of Calcutta's life also. In Bihar and U.P., there was a general trend amongst those who wanted to pursue higher education after completing schools more specifically in medicine and engineering to prefer Calcutta. Those who preferred engineering education, their favourite destination was Shibpur Engineering College, near Howrah.

People belonging to Momin-Ansar community from Uttar Pradesh had also settled in Calcutta, both for pursuing education and mostly for promotion of their business interests. The business class was mainly settled in Zakaria Street, Kolutola Street and Khidderpore areas. Handloom fabrics from Tanda, Gorakhpur and other parts of Uttar Pradesh besides Zari work of Benares had a big market in Calcutta. There were clusters of the community spread over different parts of the erstwhile Indian capital, Calcutta including Park Circus, Beg Bagan, Wellesly, Narkul Danga, Kaki Nara, Bara Bazaar, Khidderpore, Zakaria Street, Howrah, Sibpore, etc. In fact, in some areas their population was so strong that they outnumbered the Bengalis.

The Beginning

The Momin movement dates back to the beginning of the 20th century. There were a definite sign of consciousness in the community. During the period between 1913 and 1924, India witnessed awave of restlessness amongst the Ansari community for attainment of equal social status, a place of dignity in the Muslim society. Small meetings at district headquarters and state capitals were organized and pamphlets were distributed highlighting the necessity of unity in order to wipe out social evil of caste system. There were consistent efforts to organize the Momin-Ansar community primarily in Bihar, United Provinces, Delhi, Maharashtra, Central Provinces and Bengal under different banners. Researches made in this regard show that as early as in the year 1913, at an initial stage, one Qauzi Abdul Jabbar, a native of Shaikhpura in Bihar took initiative and established an organization called '*Falahul Momineen*' at a meeting held at 3, Sarat Ghosh Street, Calcutta. Qauzi Jabbar could not live long and with his death in 1915, his organization also faded away. However, the situation was saved at a meeting of the '*Jamiat Momenin*' to further the cause of the community held the same year in the mosque of Genda Talab under the presidentship of Hakim Abdul Ghani Ghazipuri. Maulana Abu Shoaib Benarsi, Maulana Abu Shoaib Khorgoi, Maulana Md. Yahya Sasarami, Editor of '*Al-Momin*', Maulvi Md. Yahya and an advocate from Shaikhpura, Bihar, Md. Yahya were present in the meeting. They picked up the thread which was left behind by Qauzi Abdul Jabbar. In the same city of Calcutta, another person named Ali Hassan, who was popularly known as Asim Bihari, and who hailed from Biharsharif, set up an organization of the Ansari community in the year 1918. This move of Asim Bihari bore fruits. In the state of Bihar, three prominent persons of the community in Patna, Maulvi Md. Zamiruddin Engineer, father of Professor Hafiz Shamsuddin of Manershrif; Hakim Maula Buksh who had established Noorani

Dawakhana in Bankipore area of Patna and built his residential place, 'Noorani Bagh' over a sprawling area with a farm of rare herbal species in East Patna, both the units still exist; and the third, a businessman from Patna City Master Md. Jaan, were collectively associated with the Momin movement in its early period. They used to hold small meetings at Shahgunj, Sultangunj, Alamgunj, Dadarmandi, Purab Darwaza and Fasahat-Ka-Maidan in Patna City area, which were then parts of the main Patna town. In the same period, the flame of the movement started burning in other parts of the state including Darbhanga, Sitamarhi, Siwan, Muzaffarpur, Purnia, Shahabad and other places. The cluster of villages, densely populated by the Momin-Ansar community in the length and breadth of Patna district including Manersharif, Rasulepure Katesar, Lai, Aain Khan, Belhouri, Nabi Nagar, Sigouri and Pali were all in the grip of movement fever. As an outcome, it was in the year 1919 that they established an organization with the name of '*Jamiat Ansarian*'. Though Jharkhand was the most backward area of the state, it did not lag behind and in the leadership of persons like Md. Ibrahim Ansari and R. Ali, besides a host of others, picked up the thread of the movement from the rest of the state with full zeal. The Momin leaders of the area organised the Momin community to march along with the rest of the country. It is worth mentioning that it was Jharkhand area from where five leaders of the Momin community won assembly seats during separate electorate in the year 1946.

In Jhajha, Bihar (now in Jharkhand) the proprietor of Swadeshi Biri Co. (estd.1904) Khan Saheb Md. Ibrahim Ansari, a very influential person of the area, held a massive conference of the Momin community in its initial days which was attended by leaders from Bihar and outside. Twenty two years later, the proprietors of Swadeshi Biri Co. held another conference of the Monghyr district Momin Conference which was inaugurated by Abdul Qaiyum Ansari and presided by Rezaur Rahman Ansari, President, Bihar Weaver's Congress. Those who attended included Dy Minister, Abul Ahad Mohammad Noor,—Hafiz Manzoor Hussain, Shams Abdul Ghafoor and Abdur Rauf Ansari of Calcutta. Abdus Sami Nadvi, MLC; Abdur Razzaque Ansari, MLC; Maulana Saminuddin, MLA; Sardar Latifur Rahman, MLA; Md. Yasin Ansari, ex-MLA of Hazaribagh; and Md. Yasin Ansari, ex-MLA of Madhupur were also present.

Initial Journals: In Calcutta, Maulvi Md. Yahya brought out '*Al Momin*' which became the mouthpiece of the Momin-Ansar community. Maulvi Asim Bihari edited '*Al-Ekram*' which also served as an organ of Momin-Ansar. In Bihar, Maulvi Md. Hafizullah brought out '*Musawaat*' from Phulwarisharif edited by Maulvi Hafizullah and Abdul Qaiyum Ansari and Al-*Momin* from Badayun, U.P. These journals exclusively dealt with the Momin movement at its earliest stage. During the same period, a number of other such journals appeared to espouse the cause of the Momin-Ansar community. All those journals almost faded away with the death of all those who were associated with them. There is perhaps not a single copy present for the community of the present generation.

Before coming to the events that led to the formal shaping of the Momin Conference, I would like to place a few notable names being the pillars of the movement. In fact, besides those whose names have been given below, there were hundreds of others who closely cooperated with these persons and richly contributed to the shaping of this great movement. Their role cannot be undermined.

Maulvi Md. Yahya and Abu Shamsh Abdul Ghafoor: At the early age of life, the author had the opportunity to develop close contacts with some of the key founders of the movement; a rare priviledge at the present time, as perhaps none other can rightly claim to have known about their heart and mind and sincerity towards the movement. They need special reference, as it was out of their collective efforts and rare show of determination that they could successfully be able to break the ice.

Maulvi Md. Yahya and Abu Shams Abdul Ghafoor, two of the founding fathers of the organization used to narrate, on different occasions, full account and spirit of the movement right from its inception.

Forefathers of Maulvi Md. Yahya came to Calcutta from Biharsharif in Bihar. Son of Haji Altaf Hussain, he was born in Calcutta in 1895. He completed his Madrasa education in Bihar. He brought out first organ of the Momin community, '*Al-Momin*' and organized the first meeting of the community in Calcutta to give shape to the movement. '*Al-Momin*' was the first magazine that aroused the Momin community to the need of the hour. It was the moving force behind the unparallel unity amongst the community members in the length and breadth of the country. He will be remembered as the most remarkable leaders of the movement.

Abu Shams Abdul Ghafoor was an affectionate man. My interest in the movement grew so much that during my frequent visits to Calcutta to see my close relations, I had made it obligatory on my part to pay a visit to ageing Shams Ghafoor in his whole sale cigarette shop in Kolu Tola area. Shams Ghafoor Saheb's name was synonym with the movement. He sacrificed his whole life for the cause of the upliftment of the community. At Calcutta, where Momin movement took its birth, he was instrumental in establishing Momin High School in Narkul Danga area, thickly populated by Momin-Ansar community with the active support of engineer Shamshuddin Ahmad and others. This education institution set up by Shams Ghafoor Saheb and other selfless people of the community six decades back, proved a boon in bringing about educational revolution in the community. During these visits, I came in contact with his cousin, Abdur Rauf Ansari a Momin Conference-Congress activist, who later became a member of West Bengal assembly and a cabinet minister. After the death of Z.R. Ansari, Abdur Rauf Ansari was elected president of the All India Momin Conference. Both of these Momin luminaries, Maulvi Md. Yahya and Shams Ghafoor survived long. It is significant to note that they were present at the 10th session of the All India Momin Conference in the year 1976, about fifty years after they had founded it, held at the sprawling Gandhi Darshan (now Indira Gandhi Indoor Stadium) on the bank of river Yamuna in Delhi that met under the chairmanship of its president and the then Union Minister, Ziaur Rahman Ansari. It was a remarkable occasion held in the gloomy background of the infamous Turkman Gate episode and proved to be the largest ever gathering of the Muslim community in Delhi after independence. Prime Minister Indira Gandhi inaugurated the national session of the All India Momin Conference.

(The Turkman Gate happenings created stir in the country. The government was being criticized by every section, especially the Muslim community for the police excesses for forced vasectomy of Muslims.)

Ali Hussain Aasim Bihari was a very good orator and had the capacity to impress his audience about the necessity and importance of organizing the Ansaris and other fellow backward Muslims to come out from the shackles of twin social malaise of slavery and inferiority complex. The beauty of Asim Bihari's speeches was that he used local dialects to create curiosity among the listeners who found great interest in his inspiring speeches and used to listen him with rapt attention. He was a small time employee but that did not deter him from carrying on with his mission. He singularly toured the length and breadth of the country and infused a new life amongst the demoralized section of the Muslim society, the Momin community. He got tremendous response wherever he went. He was known as the *'Gashti Safeer'* (Roving ambassador) of the Momin movement. Asim Bihari was beyond doubt, one of the strong pillars of the movement. To be true, he dedicated his life for the Momin community and the movement.

Professor Hafiz Shamshuddin Ahmad 'Shamsh' belonged to Maner Sharif in the district of Patna, Bihar. He graduated from Gwalior and then came back to Patna. He did his M.A. in Urdu and also, L.L.B. He was appointed a lecturer in the Government College, Muzaffarpur in 1921. Later, he was transferred to Raunesha College, Cuttack, Orissa (now Odisha) in the year 1923. A couple of years later, he presided over the first ever conference of the Momin community at Calcutta in the year 1924, which proved a launching pad of this great movement. His second transfer was from Raunesha College, Cuttack to Patna College from where he retired as HOD of Urdu. After superannuation, he lived in his house, 'Shamsh Manzil' at Shah Gunj in Patna where he expired. He was a distant relation of the author and so, had the opportunity to be in constant touch with him that gave enough opportunity to know about the movement from its early days.

Maulvi Md. Hafizullah of Phulwarisharif, Patna came from a well to do Momin family having a good organizational capacity and journalistic ability. He edited *'Musawaat'*; a very popular Urdu magazine of that period published from Phulwarisharif which occupied an important position at the early stage of Momin community's uprising. He was a close friend of my father. He was one of the few Momin personalities who fully dedicated his life to the cause of the downtrodden Momin community. He served the community through his writings *in Musawaat*. He was a noble person and came from an aristocrat family.

Hafizullah Saheb was deadly against the creation of Pakistan. After partition when his family members, under unavoidable circumstances, decided to shift to Karachi, he refused to go and preferred to stay back in Patna. It was a very difficult decision for him. His son was married to the daughter of Sayeed. A.Shaikh, Bombay, General Secretary, All India Momin Conference.

Maulvi Hafizullah was now living alone in his big mansion at Phulwarisharif.A person who was till now, living with all the available luxuries of life with his family, was now living a lonely life facing the hardship, day in and day out. Sometime later, he disposed off his house and started living in a rental accommodation in Subzibagh area of Patna which was then a hub of Urdu newspapers. He started working in some Urdu daily. During those days, I had also started my journalistic career and so we used to meet very often. Compulsions of old age made him to shift reluctantly to his family in Karachi. Even there, he worked in an English weekly of Karachi, 'Unity'. He continued to write me post cards till his death.

Md. Yahya: Incidentally, there were three Yahyas who contributed to the founding of the historical movement at Calcutta. One was Maulvi Md. Yahya, another was Shamshul Ulema Maulana Md. Yahya of Kochas, Sasaram and the third was Md. Yahya, Advocate from Shaikhpura in Bihar, who was then practicing in Calcutta. During those days when the community, due to educational backwardness, was leading a miserable life in the state, the Momin community of Shaikhpura scripted a different story. They took to education and flourished in all spheres.

Md. Yahya, Advocate came from a highly educated and reputed family. His father was Hakim Nazir Hassan. Md. Yahya had a very brilliant academic career. Later, he left Calcutta and returned back to Patna. He was appointed in the state judicial service in 1925; in 1938, he was appointed Registrar of courts. He rose to the post of Assistant Registrar of Patna High Court in 1942 and Dy Registrar in 1945.Next, he was appointed Addl. District and Sessions judge, Gaya in 1948 and within two years, he was made District and Sessions judge. He again came back to Patna High Court as Registrar. The state government appointed him as member, Bihar Public Service Commission, from where he retired.

He left behind three illustrious sons. Eldest is Dr. Mahmood Alam, a renowned surgeon of Jamshedpur; second was Dr. Masood Alam, who died a couple of years back in Austin, USA. And the third Md. Matloob has retired as Dy. Registrar, Patna High Court.

Barrister Md. Mohiuddin: Another judicial luminary and a notable figure of the Momin movement in its early days was Barrister Mohiuddin. Being from the intellectual class, he proved himself an asset for the upcoming Momin movement. The author had the opportunity to meet him at his daughter's residence in Malviya Nagar, New-Delhi. He was the first and the last chairman of the Momin Parliamentary Board set up in the year 1939.

Forefathers of Barrister Md. Mohiuddin originally belonged to Kota in Rajasthan. During Mutiny of 1857, they shifted to Benares and later to Calcutta. He studied at Calcutta and had a brilliant academic career. He wanted to compete in ICS exams. He first faced interview, as was the practice for ICS competition, but later decided not to sit in competitive examination. He decided to sail for England. After he returned from England, he practiced in Calcutta and later shifted to Tezpur, Assam where he finally settled. Barrister Mohiuddin was one of the strong pillars of the Momin movement. He was actively involved in the freedom struggle.

Momin Conference took a wise and prompt decision in its annual session held at Gorakhpur to convert, till then a social organization, into a political entity. Three prominent leaders, Shaikh Zahiruddin, Abdul Qaiyum Ansari and Barrister Mohiuddin were strongly in favour of this historic resolution to meet the challenges of Muslim League. Being the most suitable person, he was made Chairman of the Momin Parliamentary Board. Immediately after in 1940, he showed his mettle in successfully conducting its first elections of Calcutta Corporation.

Justice Iqbal Ansari, Hon'ble judge of Patna High Court is the illustrious son of Barrister Mohiuddin.

Maulana Furkhund Ali, born in Sasaram, Bihar, son of Shaikh Inayat Ali, a trader, Maulana Furkhund Ali is a prominent name of the Momin movement. He was one of the architects of this historic movement. Maulana Furkhund Ali inaugurated the second conference of Jamiat Momineen in Calcutta presided over by Maulvi Abdul Aziz Abdul Latif, M.L.C., Bombay. Back home after

Calcutta conference, Maulana Furkhund Ali adressed the community members at a meeting organized by *Anjuma-e-Ansarian,* Sasaram and apprised the audience with the proceedings of Calcutta Conference and the unprecedented enthusiasm he observed there. He spearheaded the spread of the movement in the four corners of the Arrah district.

Hakim Kabiruddin: A very prominent and noble personality of the Ansar-Momin community in Delhi whose name deserved most to be quoted here was Hakim Kabiruddin. Though he was not himself directly involved in the movement as an activist but certainly he gave moral support to those in Delhi who were in the forefront of the movement at the earlier period. He was the first amongst his generation who wanted that such a vast community of Ansaris should organize itself to bring about educational revolution in the community which, he termed, was the key to success in life. A pride of the Momin community, Hakim Kabiruddin who became a legendry figure of Unani medicine in his lifetime, originally hailed from Shaikhpura in Bihar. Hakim Kabiruddin's book 'Bayaz-e-Kabir' is an excellent collection of Unani prescriptions for all sorts of diseases which is still used extensively by the Unani practitioners even today. He served as the Principal of Delhi Tibbiya College. Another figure of Unani medicine who established Hamdard Dawakhana, a name on the tips of every Indian, was Hakim Abdul Hamid. He was a student of Hakim Kabiruddin for whom he had great respect. Hakim Abdul Hamid had provided a house for Hakim Kabiruddin for his lifetime after his retirement from service.

Hakim Mazharuddin Ajmali: Momin community had a very active person in Delhi, Hakim Mazharuddin Ajmali, who was then a very influential figure in government circles in Delhi. He was the nephew of Hakim Kabiruddin and married to Hakim Kabiruddin's daughter. Hakim Mazharuddin Ajmali lived on the back of Gali Qasim Jaan in the walled city in a spacious building with a sprawling area attached to it where he usually held Qawwali programmes of which he was very fond of. I along with Ansari Saheb met him for the first time in late fifties. Later, I used to see him to pay my respect whenever I visited Delhi. I had then started my career as a journalist at Patna. There was a vacancy in the Press Information Bureau, Government of India for which I was also an applicant. Lala Shamnath of Delhi was the Deputy Information Minister in the Union ministry. Ansari Saheb advised me to meet Ajmali Saheb. He gave me a letter in Ajmali Saheb's name requesting him to speak to Lala Sham Nath in this regard. Ajmali Saheb was quick to respond and called the Deputy Information Minister on phone with forceful plea to help me. However, it was a different matter that it could not materialize.

Maula Bukhsh Thikedar: Among other notable activists of the Momin movement of its early age I met was Maula Bux 'Thikadar' of Amroha in Delhi, a very strong leader of the movement. I met him during his last days when he was confined to bed. He lived in Gali Qasin Jaan in old Delhi. He showed me the cot lying by his side on which the 'roaming ambassador' of Momin movement, Asim Bihari used to take rest after whirlwind tour of western U.P. I personally knew another three persons of Delhi who were closely associated with Momin movement. They were Hafiz Abdul Aziz, a prominent businessman of Delhi and member Delhi Metropolitan Council who was elected as the Chairman, Reception Committee of the 10th session of Momin Conference. Others were Maulvi Habibur Rahman and Haji Fayyazuddin residing in Lal Darwaza of old Delhi. Maulvi Habibur Rahman had a small shop of watch repair in the same locality on the main road. Haji Fayyazuddin had a small manufacturing business. Both of them were dedicated to Momin movement and Congress. Like many others, I was introduced to both of them by Abdul Qaiyum Ansari. Whenever we travelled to Delhi, Ansari Saheb must make a call to both of them. They were always crazy to host Ansari Saheb. Their insistence out of love and humility was difficult to be turned down.

Istefa Hussain Ansari: In Uttar Pradesh, there were a number of Momin leaders who had sacrificed their life's for the upliftment of the Momin community and strengthening the Momin Conference. The foremost among them was Istefa Hussain Ansari of Gorakhpur, who later became a cabinet minister in that state. He was first elected member of U.P. Legislative Council in 1966.He was re-elected as MLC in 1972 and remained as MLC till 1978.In 1973, Chief Minister Haemvati Nandan Bahuguna took him in his eleven member cabinet as a cabinet minister for small industries. In March 1971, Istefa Hussain organized and led a massive rally of the weavers in support of their demands in Lucknow. This rally of the weavers of Uttar Pradesh under his leadership proved memorable that took Lucknow by storm.

His son Ashfaque Hussain Ansari became member of the 7th Lok Sabha. Among other notable Momin leaders of Uttar Pradesh were Maulana Abdul Majeed Hariri of Benares, Md. Reyazuddin, Advocate and Md. Nezamuddin, Advocate, Allahabad, Abid Ali Ansari of Sitapur and Nesar Ahmad Ansari of Tanda. Both of them became minister in the state cabinet. Other Momin leaders were Maulvi Habibur Rahman Nomani of Mau Nath Bhanjan; Md. Amin Ansari of Mau-Aaema, Allahabad, both became Rajya Sabha members; Dildar Hussain Ansari, M.L.C., Sattar Ansari, M.L.A., Bijnaur; Vakil Ansari, Hakim Hazique of Itawa; Haji Abdul Qadeer Ansari; Zahoor Bhaijan and Babu Ashfaque in Moradabad. Haji Abdul Qadeer was the first President of U.P. Momin Conference. His son Humayun Qadeer became Mayor of Moradabad. Khurshid Ahmad Ansari of Amroha was also elected to the U.P. assembly. Haji Sekhawat Din, a businessman and Abdul Qaiyum Ansari of Feelgunj were strong pillars of Momin Conference in Kanpur. Huzoor Ansari in Kareli. In Bhadohi, Ansari community of carpet industry fully supported the movement. When All India President of the Momin Conference, Abdul Qaiyum Ansari and myself visited Bhadohi in connection with organizational matters in late fifties, the proprietor of Vazir Ali & Sons, Abdul Qaiyum Ansari was the host. He was fully dedicated to the movement in U.P. Others were Ashfaque Vaziri and Naimullah Ansari.

Whenever Ansari Saheb and I went on tour to Lucknow, our itinerary always included a visit to Darul Shefa, Uttar Pradesh MLA hostel. It was the most suitable place to meet all the Momin leaders, members of both houses and others. Apart from the activities in the state office, situated nearby, the activists, as a routine, used to assemble at Darul Shefa. Flat number 27/B of Darul Shefa was the meeting place. Whenever we visited the place, we could invariably meet Ziaur Rahman Ansari and Md. Nasim Ansari.

In Karnataka Tajuddin Nawaz Bhai was the strong pillar of the Momin movement. He represented south in the national working committee.

In other states like Assam and Orissa in the east and

Maharashtra, Gujarat, Madhya Pradesh, Momin Conference was equally on a strong base. Md. Mustafa Ansari of Italian Bakery and Prof. Nesar Ahmad Ansari in Gujarat; Jalil Saaz in Nagpur, Prof. Mobin Shaikh, Hayat Ansari and Sohail Shaikh, son of former general secretary, Sayeed A. Shaikh, Engineer in Bombay, Shabbir Rahi and Yasin Ansari, Advocate in Bhiwadi, and Md. Hanif Ansari in Jabalpur, Madhya Pradesh were actively associated with the movement.

Though during that period, in Jharkhand which was then a part of Bihar, the community was both socially and educationally extremely backward but was fully alive to the movement. In fact they proved themselves more conscious of the need of the hour and scripted history in that direction. It was this area that gave maximum number of seats in the assembly during the historic elections on separate electorate in 1946. Ibrahim Ansari was the first Momin community member to be elected to Lok Sabha from Ranchi, Jharkhand. R. Ali and later Zahoor Ali were members of the state legislature and Amanat Ali in the Council. Presently, Furqan Ansari is the senior most Congress/Momin leader of the state. He is credited with five consecutive wins from his Jamtara constituency. He was a cabinet minister in the joint state of Bihar and once full time Member of Parliament from Godda. Another senior and distinguished Momin leader, Maulvi Saminuddin was twice elected to Parliament. He could not complete second term and expired. Prof. Salahuddin Ansari, son of Md. Yasin Ansari MLA, Santhal Pargana became Member Parliament from the same constituency. Mumtaz Ansari, a lecturer in the College of Commerce, Patna won parliament seat from Koderma. He was brutally murdered in mysterious circumstances which the police could not solve.

Md. Hussain Ansari from Madhupur was elected to Bihar assembly on Congress ticket. After separation as Jharkhand state, he joined JMM of Sibu Soren. He was twice cabinet minister of Jharkhand. He has since been defeated in elections. Earlier, Israel Ansari and Nezam Ansari became MLAs from Gomio and Raj Dhawar constituencies respectively.

In Delhi others worth mentioning are Sayeed Ansari, son of Maula Bux Thikedar, Md. Ibrahim Ansari of Mohallah Bara Hindu Rao, Yakub Ansari, Ballimaran and in Khuraiji, Md. Mustafa Ansari, a powerloom industry baron.

In Bihar after the death of Abdul Qaiyum Ansari, his elder son Khalid Anwer Ansari got elected from Dehri-on Sone and made minster of state. Later he resigned from Congress, joined Samata Party and then RJD. He was MLC also for three years. After the dealth of Abul Ahad Md. Noor, his only son Khalid Rashid Saba was nominated MLC and was a minister thrice under three chief ministers. He got two terms of Council membership. Chandra Sekhar Singh nominated Abdur Razzaque Ansari to the Legislative Council and was appointed a minister in Jagannath Mishra cabinet. Md. Hussain Ansari of Aurangabad and Fida Hussain Ansari from Darbhanga were also MLCs.

Prof. Ashfaque Ansari MLA from Darbhanga, was minister in the state cabinet. Shakiluzzaman, son of Haji Noorul Hoda of Patna won assembly elections from Biharshrif. He was appointed Dy. Minister under S.N. Sinha. However, he could not make it for the second time. Aas. Md. Ansari was elected to Parliament from Siwan.

Shaping of the Organization

The efforts initiated as early as in the year 1913 by the Momin activists in Calcutta took formal shape in January, 1924 when a meeting was organized in the house of hide merchant Karamat Hussain at 11, Damzan Lane in the Park Circus area of Calcutta city under the chairmanship of Ali Ahmad Buland Akhtar, a leading hide merchant of Calcutta who hailed from Bhagalpur. It was in this meeting that *Jamiatul Momeneen,* Calcutta was finally established. A group of Ansari intellectuals were collectively the convenors of the meet with the main objective that the meeting becomes successful and not a flop. Every individual had the responsibility to bring with him a person or two in the meeting. Incidentally, among the convenors, there were three 'Yahyas'. Maulana Md. Yahya (Shamsul Ulema) hailed from Kochas, in the district of Sasaram, Bihar. Maulana was head teacher in Calcutta's famed Madarsa Alia. His son Hafiz Manzoor Hussain became M.L.A in Bihar after independence. Another Md. Yahya, an advocate was from Sheikhpura, Bihar. The third, Maulvi Yahya was the real brain behind the meet. He had a small hand press. The invitation for the meeting was printed by Maulvi Yahya himself in all secrecy, with precautions that the news about the meet does not leak and the very first meeting may not become a target for unnecessary controversy. Invitations were sent to known and selective persons of the Momin community. Besides them, other prominent persons who attended the meeting included Ali Ahmad Buland Akhtar; Abul Hassan Kashif, M.A.; Bismil Arvi, B.A.; Abu Shams Abdul Ghafoor; and Asim Bihari. There was an unprecedented response from the Momins of Calcutta. Beyond expectations, large number of people, more than those invited, came to the meeting to listen about the strategy being adopted to organize the vast but unorganized Momin community. It proved a great success, both in terms of attendance and deliberations. There were noticeable thrill and excitement as every person attending the meet was now confident that something concrete shall take place and definite steps will follow to wipe out the evil of caste system prevailing in the Muslim society.

This meeting turned out to be the turning point in the lives of the largest section of the Indian Muslims, the Ansaris. The effort of the persons who organized the historic meet was appreciated by the Momin community. The message reached the length and breadth of the country. It generated excitement. In less than a year, such meetings were organized in Delhi, Central Provinces, United Provinces, Bihar and Bombay. In Calcutta itself, small meetings were held in places like Narkul Danga, Khidderpore, Park Circus, Tanti Bagan, Bau Bazar and other places. Maulvi Md. Yahya, Asim Bihari, Shamsuddin Ahmad, Engineer, Maulvi Shahiduddin, a bakery owner and Abu Shams Abdul Ghafoor, spearheaded the movement in Calcutta in its early days. Contribution of Shams Abdul Ghafoor in organizing the Momin movement is of great significance. He was a dedicated person to the cause of Ansaris. He stressed the need to give priority to education. He along with Master Shamshuddin of Tanti Bagh and Alhaj Engineer Shamshuddin were instrumental in establishing Momin High School in Narkul Danga well before the movement took its formal shape.

During the same period, prominent persons of the Momin community in different parts of the country also took initiative in organizing the Momin-Ansar community. The most significant aspect of the movement was that persons coming from every level—educated or illiterate, rich or poor, businessmen, servicemen belonging to any class—all were a part of the movement. Shaikh Murtaza Hassan of Gorakhpur; Shaikh Zahiruddin, Advocate of Ambala, Punjab; Maulvi Md. Aslam, Lahore; Munshi Azimullah, Dehra Doon; Shaikh Maula Buksh Thekadar of Amroa; Md. Sulaiman, M.L.C., Calcutta; and Abdus Sattar Farooqui, Kamti, Maharashtra were all active in their own areas. Sayeed Shaikh Engineer, Abdul Aziz Abdul Latif, M.L.C., Abdur Rahman Feet Wala (Kurla) and Md. Umar Rajjab (Madanpura) were spearheading the movement in Maharashtra. It is worth noting that Md. Umar Rajjab was the first from the Momin-Ansari community to represent India at the world labour conference in Geneva, Australia.

First conference of the Calcutta Jamiatul Momeneen was held in the town hall at Calcutta on March 22 and 23, 1925. This was the formal setting up of the Momin movement. Professor Hafiz Shamshuddin, Professor of Urdu, Raonesha College, Cuttack, presided over the meet. He hailed from Manersharif, near Patna and came from an affluent family. He was a descendant of Momin Arif. He got his education at Gwalior in Madhya Pradesh. He was first appointed as a lecturer in government college, Muzaffarpur. He was transferred to Raonesha College, Cuttack in 1923 and was finally transferred to Patna University from where he retired.

Writing his memoir in the '*Sada-e-Hind*' Urdu weekly of Patna, Professor Hafiz Shamshuddin narrated the enthusiasm of the members of the Momin community. When he alighted from train at the Howrah station, he was profusely garlanded and taken out in a procession to the venue of the conference. The enthusiasm of the participants was indicative of the determination of the community to march ahead with firm resolve.

Developments were taking place in a fast pace. In Calcutta itself, inspired by the success of the first session of the Jamiatul Momeneen, smaller units at places like Belgachia, Howrah, Manik Tollah, Kolu Tola and Machua Bazar were formed. It quickly spread over to the different parts of the country as well. In Allahabad, Bijnor, Moradabad, Kashipore, Sitapore, Naini Taal, Sadhura, Amritsar, Biharsharif, Patna, Sasaram, Darbhanga, Bhagalpur-branches of Jamiatul Momeneen were established.

Second session of the Calcutta Jamiatul Momeneen was held at Holiday Park on December 25 and 26, 1926. It was inaugurated by Maulana Furkhund Ali of Sasaram and presided over by Maulvi Abdul Latif Abdul Aziz, M.A, L.L.B; M.L.C, Dhulia, Western Khandes. Though it was a state level conference from all accounts, it presented a picture of a national meet. Momin leaders and workers from different parts of the country made it a point to attend the Calcutta conference. Maulvi Abdul Baqui who was to preside, could not make it to the conference.Hence in his absence, Maulvi Abdul Latif Abdul Aziz presided. Shamshuddin Ahmad, Counsellor, Calcutta Corporation was the chairman of the reception committee.

A large number of delegates from Bihar, U.P. and other places attended the second session of the Calcutta Jamiatul Momeneen. Prominent among those were Md. Nezamuddin, Advocate, Allahabad; Maulana Imamuddin Ram Nagri, Benaras, Editor, *'Momin Ansar'*; Hafizullah, Gorakhpur; Maulana Shakoor Ahmad, Mubarakpur, Azamgardh; Maulvi Ali Hussain Asim Bihari, Editor, *'Al-Ekram'*, Biharshrif; Maulana Farkhund Ali, Sasaram; Dr. Moniruddin and Md. Salim Ansari, Advocate, Bhagalpur; Maulvi Nurul Hoda, Noorani Dawakhana, Patna; Maulvi Hafiz Abdul Karim, Maroof Gunj, Gaya; M.A. Hanif, Aligarh; Maulana Abu Shoaib Md. Ismael from Delhi; and Maulana Md. Yasin Nazim.

By now the movement had gained momentum and it was fast marching ahead. With the ad hoc formation of the organization at national level, there was growing demand from the provinces to hold national session in order to give formal shape to the new organization.

There was an urgent desire to hold the first session of the Momin Conference at Calcutta itself as the city had become synonym with the movement. Calcutta had witnessed very successful two state level sessions of the Momin Conference within the gap of only two years that had generated hope and aspiration amongst the members of the community throughout the country. The tremendous success of the Calcutta conference led to formal announcement of the establishment of All India Momin Conference. It was decided to have its headquarters at Calcutta itself for the present. It was resolved to fix number of persons to be elected for the managing committee which were as follows:

Madras-3; Central Provinces-4; Bombay state-6; Punjab-5; U.P.-1; Bengal-10; Bihar-10; Calcutta Presidency-10; Ajmer, Rajputana-3; and Hydrabad Deccan-3.

> *Office-bearers*: *President*: Maulana Haji Farkhund Ali from Sasaram, Bihar; *General Secretary*: Ali Ahmad Buland Akhtar, Bhagalpur, Bihar; *Jt. Secretary*: Maulana Md Ibrahim, Darbhanga, Bihar; *Assistant Secretaries*: Maulvi Md. Akbar, Allahabad, Maulvi Md. Shafi, B.A., L.L.B, Ghazipuri (all U.P.), Master Hemayat Hussain, Calcutta; *Treasurer*: Abdus Shakoor.

The working committee was formed generously large to accommodate all prominent activists from across the country. Prominent those included were Maulana Imamuddin Ramnagri and Md. Nezamuddin, Advocate from U.P.; Khan Bahadur Abdul Jalil, Advocate; Ali Hussain Asim Bihari, Professor Hafiz Shamshuddin and Maulvi Md. Hafizullah from Bihar; Maulvi Abdul Aziz, M.L.C. from Bombay.

1st Session of All India Momin Conference, Calcutta 1928

The much awaited first session of the newly formed All India Momin Conference was held at Holiday Park in Calcutta on April 7 and 8, 1928, only after a gap of two years of the second state level session.

Maulana Abdul Majeed Hariri, from Benaras presided over the session. Maulana Hariri was a great scholar and had command over seven languages. After India became an independent nation, Hariri was appointed ambassador at Jeddah, Saudi Arabia. With his scholarly address and oratory excellence, he was able to give new direction to the community. Maulana Hariri called upon the community to shed inferiority complex and stressed the prime need for education. He forcefully decried those interested quarters within the Muslim community who had smuggled in caste system and had divided Muslims in the categories of 'Shareef' and 'Razeel'. Tens of thousands of the members of the Momin community representing different parts of the country had poured into the city of Calcutta. The first national session of the All India Momin Conference proved a milestone in the history of the community. It had generated so much interest in the social and political arena that the prominent Muslim League leader of Bengal, Hasan Shaheed Suhrawardy took the opportunity to attend the session. He was sitting on the dais as one of the invited dignitaries. After the formation of Pakistan, Suhrawardy became one of its Prime Ministers. This conference left a deep impression on the Indian politics.

The first session of the Momin Conference proved to be a moral booster for the Momin-Ansari who had been living a life of humiliation within the Muslim community.

2nd Session of All India Momin Conference, Allahabad 1929

Every member of the Momin-Ansar community living anywhere in the country welcomed formation of their own organisation which kindled a new hope in their hearts that, with unity among the community members demonstrated at the first session, it will be possible for them to come out from the shackles of a miserable life and a new era of social, educational and economic uplift will don their lives. Inspired by the grand success of national conference held at Calcutta, and the enthusiasm displayed, Momin leaders of U.P. decided to hold 2nd national conference somewhere in their state. In June, 1928, the Working Committee of the All India Momin Conference was called at Mohalla Atala in Allahabad to discuss the issue. It was finally decided to hold the conference on March 30 and 31, 1929 at the sprawling Khusro Bagh in Allahabad. A reception committee with Shaikh Ali Hussain as its chairman was formed. Shaikh Mohammad Zahiruddin, Advocate from Ambala, Punjab was invited to preside over the session.

Preliminary preparations to hold the session started immediately after. The foremost task was to ensure well in advance, the booking of Khusro Bagh, the historical place selected for holding the session which was under the care of superintendent, horticulture, Mr. Smith. Mr. Nezamuddin Advocate of Allahabad High Court took the responsibility and could be able to get the required permission subsequently.

Shaikh Zahiruddin was given a tumultous welcome when he arrived at Allahabad railway station at 2 p.m. on March 29.

Dignitaries of the Momin community in Allahabad profusely garlanded him and was taken in a procession to the house of Master Abdur Razaqque who had offered to host the President and other dignitaries from Calcutta, Bihar and Punjab.

On the preparation side, a very huge and decorated Pandal was erected at the venue to accommodate thousands of delegates. Munshi Rahmatullah, Hafiz Md. Ibrahim, Shamim Bux, Md. Shafi and Hafiz Rasool Bux supervised the erection of Pandal and seating arrangements. A volunteer force was set up with younger group from Atala Chawk, Garhi, Bahadur Gunj, Dondipore, Daryabad, Mirapur and other localities of Allahabad town. Shaikh Md. Akbar, Secretary; Anjuman Shabul Ansar, Hafiz Md. Siddique, Secretary; Anjuman Tanzeemul Ansar and Munshi Abdul Karim alias Bahauddin, Secretary-*Hidayatul Muslemin,* were in the forefront in organizing the volunteers.

The session started with recitation of holy Quran by Qauri Md. Wali. Before the deliberations started, national songs were sung by Master Md. Hanif son of Shaikh Md. Salim and Master Mohibullah son of Haji Abdul Hameed.

In his speech, Shaikh Murtaza Hussain stressed the need to form primary cooperative societies of the handloom weavers to give flip to the traditional handloom industry which was the mainstay of the weavers. Since he was suffering from sore throat, Md. Nezamuddin, Advocate, Allahabad read his speech.

Before the formal beginning of the session, Md. Nezamuddin moved a resolution suggesting the name of Shaikh Zahiruddin to preside over the session which was seconded by Professor Hafiz Shamsuddin, Lecturer, Patna College, Maulvi Md Yahya, Editor, *'Al-Momin"*, Calcutta and Zafar Ahmad, Advocate, Ambala.

President Shaikh Md. Zahiruddin said that the Momin-Ansari community lacked political conciousness without which all round development of the community was not possible. He stressed that political vision takes a person or a community to great heights.

3rd Session of All India Momin Conference, Delhi 1931

Within a gap of two years, the 3rd session of the Momin Conference was held at Delhi on October 17, 18 and 19, 1931. Khan Saheb

Sardar Md. Islam, Honorary Magistrate of Nagmatia, Gaya presided over the session. The third annual session was held at Hasan Manzil. For the stopover of outside guests, the spacious space of the Zeenat Mahal and a number of rooms in Lal Kuan, Ballimaran, Frashkhana Gali, Chabuk Sawaran and Katra Ghulam Mohammad were arranged by Maula Bux Thikadar and his friends. A considerable number of volunteers from Moradabad and Amroha had arrived. It was for the first time that two hundred women delegates attended the session.A large number of delegates from Burma, Bihar, Rohielkhand and Agra, Punjab, Malegaon and Bombay Central attended Delhi session. Prominent persons who regretted their absence due to unforeseen reasons included Maulana Imammuddin Ramnagri, Editor *"Turjuman Momin Ansar"*, Hakim Maula Bux of Noorani Dawakhana, Patna and Shaikh Murtaza Hussain, Municipal Commissioner and Member, District board, Gorakhpur.

The president began his speech with obitual reference to Maulana Md. Ali who had expired the same year. He exhorted the Momins to initiate a movement for spreading education which was key to the success of any community. Sardar Islam appreciated those skilled weavers who were engaged in traditional weaving profession but, as he maintained, they should provide education to their children to explore other avenues for a prosperous life and to come up to the level of others.

The president told the gathering that the leaders of the Momin-Ansar community who, just a few years back, took a historical decision at Calcutta to stand up on their feet with self confidence and organized Momin Conference is commendable that shall go down in the history as one of the most viable mass organisation. He struck a note of optimism that with the present show of unity, the community will be able to overcome all hurdles coming in the way of the movement. He advised the leadership to bring out a national organ of the Momin Conference. Sardar Islam laid emphasis on education and said that all the problems and evils related to the community were entirely due to lack of education. The only remedy lies in educating children which will bring a sea change in a few years only.

Further details of the third session at Delhi including the people responsible for holding the session, the reception committee and its chairman and the venue where it was held could not be found out from the available records.

4th Session of All India Momin Conference, Lahore 1933

Momin Conference which started its journey from Bengal reached Punjab. Five years after the first session at Calcutta, Lahore in Punjab became the venue of the fourth session of All India Momin Conference. The three day session was held on April 14, 15 and 16, 1933, under the presidentship of Shaikh Md. Murtaza Hussain, Municipal Commissioner from Gorakhpur. Shaikh Md. Zahiruddin, President of Ambala Municipal Board headed the reception committee.

In his welcome speech, Shaikh Zahiruddin made a pointed reference to the need to convert Momin Conference into a political body as he observed that without having a political base, the community cannot make effective strides in different fields. It was he who was mainly instrumental in getting Momin Conference ultimately converted into a politcal organisation a few years after in the seventh national session held at Gorakhpur in the year 1939.

He paid tributes to the Momin leaders especially from Bihar and Bengal whose efforts could made it possible that the community could get a viable organisation. He said that these leaders had to burn midnight oil to finally set up Momin Conference after years of efforts. The very fact that the movement has travelled from Bengal to Punjab in a consistent manner is enough indication of its viability and success in future also. He called upon the affluent members of the community to contribute generously to set up a central office of the All India Momin Conference.

Shaikh Murtaza Hussain was a socio-political activist from Gorakhpur. He held the position of a Municipal Commissioner. He came from a poor family and struggled into prominence as one of the dignitaries of Gorakhpur. His son Istafa Hussain became a cabinet minister in U.P. after independence. His grandson, Ashfaque Hussain Ansari became a Member of Parliament.

In his brilliant speech delivered from the presidential chair, Shaikh Murtaza Hussain commended the efforts of the Momin leaders of Bihar and Bengal for giving the gift of a viable organisation like the Momin Conference to the Momin-Ansar community. He decried those sections within the Indian Muslim community who had divided the Muslim community on caste basis on the pattern of the Hindu community. He further stressed that Momin Conference came into being primarily to fight against the un-Islamic practice of caste system in the Muslim community in the subcontinent and to bring about cohesion within the community. He said that since it will be a noble service to the cause of Islam, God will bestow success in this mission.

The president presented the list of members of the next working committee. The new list included—

> *President*: Shaikh Murtaza Hussain. *Senior Vice-president*: Shaikh Md. Zahiruddin, Ambala. *Vice-Presidents*: Babu Md. Hussain, Punjab; Shaikh Maula Bukhsh, Government Contractor, Amroha; Prof. Abdul Majeed, Shah Gunj, Patna; Saith Abdur Rahman; Feeta Wala, Kurla, Bombay; *General Secretary*: Md. Zafar, Advocate, Ambala; *Jt. Secretary*: Ali Hussain Asim Bihari; *Asst. Secretary*: Munshi Allah Dutta Asi, Lahore.
>
> Prominent members of the 15-member working committee were Md. Nezamuddin, Advocate, Allahabad; Maulvi Md. Hafizullah, Phulwari Sharif, Patna; Sardar Md. Islam, Hon. Magistrate, Nagmatia, Gaya; Abdul Latif Abdul Aziz, Advocate, MLC Bombay; and Md. Salman, MLC, Bengal.

5th Session of All India Momin Conference, Gaya, 1934

The fifth session of the All India Momin Conference was held at Gaya in 1934 on November 10, 11 and 12. It was the year that Bihar was hit by the worst form of earthquake that shattered the life of the state. Md. Nezamuddin Advocate, Allahabad High Court and a front rank leader of Momin movement presided. Sardar Latifur Rahman Nagmatia was elected president of the reception committee. Md. Nezamuddin was appointed Assistant Pleader to the Allahabad High Court in 1938.

Bihar had suffered immensely by earthquake and floods, but despite these odds, there was great excitement and enthusiasm amongst the organisers of the session. To facilitate preparations, different sub committees were formed. A huge pandal was set up that accommodated about two thousand important personalities. A different enclosure was prepared for ladies. Young and smart volunteers paid attention to serve the invitees. A small town of tents to accommodate the delegates was erected. Best of hotel accommodation were requisitioned for the stay of VIP invitees.

One of the most distinguished invitees was Syed Md. Abdul Aziz, Bar-at-Law, Minister of Education, Bihar and Orissa. He was accorded befitting reception at the Gaya railway station. Other dignitaries who attended the Gaya session included District Magistrate, Gaya, Babu Lakhmi Narayan Singh; Kunwar Saheb, Maharaja of Tikari, Chairman, District and Municipal Boards; Syed Hassan Imam, Member, Council of States; Khan Bahadur Syed Mahboob Alam and others.

After the presidential address, Education Minister of Bihar, Syed Abdul Aziz, Bar-at-law gave a memorable speech that was heard with both attention and interest. He appreciated the activities of the Momin Conference and said that in Islam there is nothing like upper and lower castes and decried those in the Muslim society who practiced caste system in Muslim society. Maulana Shafi Dawoodi, President, All India Muslim Conference who could not attend the meet sent a well worded exhaustive message wishing the conference a grand success. In his message, Dawoodi praised the Momin Conference for spearheading movement for the economic emancipation of the poor and downtrodden section of the Muslim society. He had high appreciation for the efforts of the Momin community to bring about Islamic brotherhood "*Musawaat*" in the society. He called upon Muslims in general to cooperate wholeheartedly with the Momin Conference in its noble mission.

Other prominent personalities who sent their messages to wish included Khan Bahadur Maulana Md. Mobarak Karim, Superintendent, Islamic Studies, Bihar and Orissa; Shaikh Md. Zahiruddin Advocate, Ambala, President, All India Momin Conference; Ghazi Mahmood Dhrampal, Commissioner, Tirhut Division; C.T. Brett, C.I.E, Dy. Inspector General, Police; Sterdeih, Rai Bahadur Charoo Chandra Mukherjee etc. On the first day at 7 p.m., Seeratun Nabi was held. Maulana Hakim Abdur Rahman, Dumraon, Maulana Hafiz Qauri Usman, Darbhanga and Maulana Haji Md. Yaqub, Khatib, Jama Masjid, Kagnara, Calcutta made speeches on the life of Prophet Mohammad. Chairman of the reception committee, Sardar Latifur Rahman Nagmatia introduced dignitaries present to the audience. Asim Bihari gave a resume of the programme on the 1st day of the session.

The session was to start formally at 11.30 a.m. but well before, all accommodation was full. Mr. Nezamuddin began his speech with reference to the earthquake that devastated Bihar and brought miseries for the people of the state. He, however, praised the courage and conviction of the organisers, who undettered, dared to hold the conference despite the havoc created by the national calamity.

In his well thought and balanced speech, Mr. Nezamuddin, turning to that section of the Muslims who believed in caste system and un-Islamic classification of 'Shareef' and 'Razeel' categories, said that the Momin Conference was not against any person or section but strongly stood against any adulteration in Islamic Shariah and advocated 'Akhoowat', the basic spirit of Islam. He said that Momin Conference will work for unity among different sections of the Muslim community.

Ali Hussain Asim Bihari, the firebrand Momin activist with his oratory skill spellbound the audience. Chairman of the reception committee, Sardar Latifur Rahman Nagmatia moved the motion of thanks. He expressed thanks to the president who could so kindly find time from his professional schedule to grace the occasion at the historic city of Gaya. He also had words of great appreciation for the different sub-committees which worked tirelessly and in a most coordinate manner to make the session successful.

The Gaya session of the AIMC constituted a sub-Committee to redraft constitution of the AIMC with Sardar Latifur Rahman, as its secretary. Other members nominated included Maulana Md. Yahya, Editor; Maulvi Md. Hafizullah, Editor, 'Musawaat', Phulwarisharif; Md. Sulaiman, MLC, Bengal; Ali Hussain Asim Bihari; Md. Akbar, Allahabad; and Maulvi Md. Abdul Majeed, Buxar, Bihar. Through another resolution every member of the Ansari-Momin community was called upon to become a member of Momin Conference by paying a membership fee of four annas annually.

The Gaya session also constituted a new working committee and nominated office—bearers of the All India Momin Conference. The following were the office-bearers:

President: Md. Nezamuddin, Advocate, Allahabad. *Vice-Presidents*: Presidents of all the State Momin Conference. *Gen. Secretary*: Sardar Latifur Rahman Nagmatia. *Jt. Secretaries*: Ali Hussain Asim Bihari, Biharshrif and Maulvi Md. Hafizullah, Phulwarishrif. *Asst. Secretary*: Maulvi Md. Ishaque, MLA, Advocate. *Treasurer*: Haji Abdul Karim, Gaya.

Working Committee: Md. Nezamuddin, Advocate, Allahabad; Sardar Md. Islam Nagmatia, Hon. Magistrate, Gaya; Sardar Latifur Rahman Nagmatia, Gaya; Khan Bahadur Mobarak Karim and Ali Hussain Asim Bihari, Biharsharif; Haji Abdul Karim, Gaya; M.G. Rasool, Calcutta; Shaikh Murtaza Hussain, Gorakhpur; Hakim Md. Bux, Municipal Commissioner, Agra; Hakim Hazique, Itawa; Md. Akbar, Atala, Allahabad; Hakim Md. Siddique, Pratapgadh; Babu Ghulam Rasool, Timber Merchant, Moradabad; Abdul Aziz Abdul Latif, MLC, Dhulia, Maharashtra; Seth Hafiz Rasool Bux, Bombay; Umar Hassan, Advocate, Bombay; Sayeed Hayat, Kanpur; Abdus Sattar, Editor 'Umeed' Kamti, Nagpur; Abu Shams Abdul Ghafoor, Calcutta; Maulvi Md. Yahya, Editor, 'Al-Momin', Calcutta; Md. Sulaiman, MLC, Bengal; Md. Zafar, Advocate, Ambala; Maulvi Abdul Majeed, Buxar; Maulvi Md. Hafizullah, Phulwarishrif; Khawja Md.Advocate, Hazaribagh; Munshi Abdul Ghani, Gaya; and Munshi Allah Dutta Aasi, Editor 'Ansari', Lahore.

6th Session of All India Momin Conference, Kanpur 1937

After Allahabad, another city of U.P., Kanpur hosted the 6th session of the All India Momin Conference on October 9, 10 and 11, 1937. It was held in the spacious campus of Halim Muslim High School. Shaikh Abdul Latif Abdul Aziz, MLC of Maharashtra who had presided over the second session of the Calcutta Jamiatul Momineen in the year 1926, was also the president of this national session.

Since its inception, Shaikh Abdul Aziz, was deeply involved in the Momin movement that was being spearheaded to ameliorate the economic and educational conditions of the community. In his fluent chaste Urdu speech, supplemented with Persian couplets to the delight of the audience, he called upon the Ansaris to give priority to education without which any individual or community will ever be successful in life. He expressed his regrets that *'Al-Momin'* edited by Maulvi Md. Yahya and which played a significant role in mobilising Ansaris to organise themselves under the roof of Momin Conference, had lately siezed its publication. He, however, commended the sincere efforts in bringing out *'Musawaat'*, *'Al-Afkar'*, *'Momin Gazette'* and *'Ansari Dunya'* which were doing their job in their respective areas. He stressed the need to bring out a newspaper at national level which could work as the mouthpiece of Momin Conference.

Kanpur session proved to be a milestone for the Momin Conference. The Momin-Ansaris all over, had by then, organised themselves through formation of Momin Conference or *Jamiatul Momineen or Jamiatul Ansar* at state and district levels. Though they had organised under different names they were all united under the umbrella of All India Momin Conference.

Kanpur session of the All India Momin Conference was one of the most successful sessions. 2500 delegates from Punjab, Bombay, Bihar, Bengal, Central Provinces, Burma and Gujarat attended the session. Out of 80,000 participants, 20,000 were women who attended different sessions.

Following persons were nominated as office-bearers to the All India Momin Conference:

> *President*: Abdul Aziz, Advocate, Dhulia (Maharashtra); *Vice-Presidents*: Presidents of all the states; *General Secretary*: A. Sayeed Shaikh, Engineer Bombay; *Jt. Secretaries*: Asim Bihari and Md. Omar, Bombay; *Assistant Secretary*: Hakim Shabir Ahmad, Jahangirabadi; *Treasurer*: Mufti Abdul Aziz Thekadar, Kanpur.
>
> *Working Committee:* Bengal and Calcutta: Prof. Senaullah, Maulana Md. Yahya, Editor, *'Al-Momin'*, Abu Shams Abdul Ghafoor, Mohiuddin, Bar-at Law, Md. Sulaiman, MLC. Bihar: Khan Saheb Md. Sardar, Nagmatia, Gaya; Sardar Latifur Rahman, Nagmatia, Gaya; Professor Hafiuz Shamsuddin, Patna; Maulvi Md. Hafizullah, Phulwarisharif; Maulana Abdul Karim, Gaya; R. Ali, MLA, Ranchi. U.P.
>
> Md. Nezamuddin, Advocate, Allahabad; Hakim Hazique, Etawah; Sardar Md. Akbar, Allahabad; Maulvi Ehsanullah, President, Panch Court, Maunath Bhanjan; Dr. Abdur Razzaque, Allahabad; Shaikhullah, Bux, Moradabad;

Munshi Md. Hassan, Mauaema, Shah Sultan Ahmad, Kanpur; Hakim Md. Siddique Zubair, Pratapgarh. Delhi: Shaikh Maula Bux Thekadar, Gali Qasim Jaan, Delhi. Punjab: Md. Zafar, Advocate, Ambala and Allah Dutta Aasi Ansari, Editor, 'Ansari' Lahore. Nagpur: Haji Abdul Qadir and Abdus Samad, Thekadar. Bombay: Abdur Rahman, Feetawale; Seth Abdus Samad, Bhiwandi; Sardar Md. Yaqub; Md. Umar, Lal Md. Abdul Ghani Sardar, Dhulia; Seth Ahmad; and Abdur Razzaque, Akola.

Political atmosphere of the country was flaming up. The Indian National Congress basically under the leadership of trio: Gandhi, Maulana Abul Kalam Azad and Pandit Jawahar Lal Nehru, had spearheaded the freedom movement with the entire nation behind. However, the Indian Muslim League headed by the trio: Md. Ali Jinnah, Liaquat Ali Khan, the second in command and Abdur Rab Nishtar, representing the elite Muslims of the country but always claimed to represent the entire Muslim community, had taken a sectarian path. Muslim League stood for a separate homeland for the Indian Muslims.

The sixth session of the Momin Conference at Kanpur proved to be momentous in more than one sense. The history began to take its natural course swiftly. At this juncture of the Indian history, Momin Conference fully geared itself to play a very difficult but decisive role for Madre Watan that ultimately formed a rich part of India's freedom struggle. The Momin community under the banner of All India Momin Conference fought on two fronts, one against the colonial rule and also, against Muslim League's demand for a separate homeland.

A.Q. Ansari's Political Career

Under the Govt. of India Act of 1935, in early 1937, assembly elections were to be held under separate electorate. Sidheshwari Prasad Sinha of Dehri-on-Sone was a noble person and very close to Abdul Qaiyum Ansari. He wanted to introduce young Ansari in politics. By then, the AIMC had not formally decided to enter electoral arena. Sidheshwari Babu prevailed upon Ansari to apply for a Muslim League ticket to contest elections from Patna. Ansari was reluctant but could not afford to turn down his proposal. However, as expected, Ansari's application was aggressively turned down by the Muslim League for obvious reason. His application was rejected and Syed Jafar Imam, general secretary of provincial Muslim League got the ticket. Out of political strategy, Sidheshwari Prasad Sinha advised Ansari to contest the elections as an independent candidate knowing well that he would loose the election since he was new in state politics. Sidheshwari Babu wanted that Ansari, in any case, should begin his political career. However, family sources of Hakim Haji Noor, proprietor of the famed 'Norani Dawakhana' told me a story related to Ansari's candidature. As the story goes, Haji Noor was the treasurer of the provincial Muslim League of which S.M. Ismail alias Hajjan Nawab was the president. On the eve of the assembly elections on separate electorate, Hajjan Nawab asked Haji Noor whether he knew any young and educated person from Ansari community since he wanted to field him in the ensuing elections. Haji Noor talked to Sultan Ahmad, Editor *'Ittehad'* who was a tenant in Haji Noor's Subzibagh house. Sultan Ahmad knew Abdul Qaiyum Ansari very well and considered him the best candidate. In the meantime, Haji Noor conveyed Hajjan Nawab that he had a talk with one A.Q. Ansari of Dehri who is ready to contest elections but from Patna itself. Ansari in Patna, Haji Noor told him to meet Hajjan Nawab with his reference. When Ansari visited S.M. Ismail's residence, he was inside with his family. He asked the person at the door to inform Hajjan Saheb that Abdul Qaiyum Ansari had come from Dehri. Muslim League president who was listening Ansari's words burst into rage and shouted, *"In Julahon Ka Damagh Kharab Ho Gaya Hai kai Nawabon Kai Shahar Sai Election Larna Chatai Hain"* (These Julahas have lost mental balance, they want to fight elections from the city of Nawabs). The Muslim League president never expected that a young boy of the Momin community would dare to ask for a ticket from state capital itself. Moreover, Hajjan wanted to field a person from the Momin community from any remote constituency not favourable to ML only as a strategy to weaken the unity of the community against M.L. Ansari could overhear his words. By the time Hajjan Nawab came out, Ansari had left the place in a huff. He came straight to Haji Noor and expressed his indignation over Nawab's humilitating comments. After this incident, it is said that Haji Noor resigned from Muslim League. Renowned historian Papiya Ghosh in her book 'Community and Nation' corroborated this story by giving reference to Momin

Conference election pamphlet in 1945 which recalled that when A.Q. Ansari had contested the Muslim League candidate in 1938 Patna bye-election, S.M.Ismail of the Muslim League expressed his unconcealed horror at a *'Julaha'* trying to get elected from the city of Nawabs.

The decision of Sidheshwari Prasad Sinha was timely that bore political fruits. This unfortunate happening proved blessing in disguise not merely for Ansari but for the entire Momin community. Ansari was now determined to enter political arena and sail against the tide. He decided to strengthen the Momin movement politically for which he was already working and threw his entire weight for the cause.

In the background of political changes coming up fast, A.Q. Ansari was elected president of the provincial Momin conference. Another Momin leader from Gaya, Sardar Latifur Rahman, son of Sardar Islam, who was a staunch supporter of Muslim League, did not accept Ansari's election on the plea of alleged election irregularities and declared himself as the president of the other faction of Bihar Momin Conference. This caused a clear division of Momin leaders of the state belonging to the Muslim League and those opposed to it.

The issue came up before the working committee of the All India Momin Conference at Kanpur. On the eve of the national session, the issue was discussed at length in the working committee meeting. Fiery speeches were made from both sides justifying the validity of claims of their respective leaders. Incidentally, Sardar Latifur Rahman did not attend the meeting on the ground of his ill health. The lively debate on the issue was a clear pointer to the fact that the Momin movement that had travelled only a short distance after its inception was fully throbbing with enthusiasm in the community. The dilemma ended when the working committee announced its decision in favour of Abdul Qaiyum Ansari. This came as a great boon to Ansari and a leap forward for the Momin Movement.

It is worth noting that while the overwhelming majority of community members in Bihar were opposed to Muslim League for more than one reason, atleast three top Momin Leaders of the province namely Sardar Latifur Rahman (Gaya), Khan Bahadur Mubarak Karim (Biharshrif) and Khan Bahadur Abdul Jalil, Advocate (Darbhanga) stood their ground and never betrayed

Muslim League. But despite this political difference, all of them without any exception were in complete solidarity with A.Q. Ansari for his social struggle through Momin Conference for the upliftment of this downtrodden community.

7th Session of the All India Momin Conference, Gorakhpur 1939

By the time the All India Momin Conference held its 7th session, the political situation of the country had warmed up. The leaders of the Momin community did not favour the idea of a separate homeland and staunchly believed in total independence of the nation. In their opinion, division of the country on communal lines was highly detrimental to the Hindu-Muslim unity and could prove danger for the integrity and stability of the country. The Momin leadership made up their mind to oppose the dangerous move of the Muslim League and totally favoured the freedom movement of the Indian National Congress which was based on Hindu-Muslim unity.

In this political background, the 7th national session of All India Momin Conference was held at Gorakhpur, eastern U.P. on December 26, 27 and 28, 1939 at Lal Diggi Park. Rayazuddin Ahmad, Advocate, Allahabad was the chairman of the reception committee and Sheikh Zahiruddin, Advocate, Ambala presided. Rayazuddin, Advocate alongwith Abdul Qaiyum Ansari had met British Labour M.P. Sir Staffords Crips of the famed historical 'Crips Mission' to present the case of the Momin community. It is worth mentioning here that the Muslim League leaders and a section of the Congress Muslims also, made an unmindful hue and cry over Ansari leaders meeting with Staffords Crips alongwith Jawahar Lal Nehru. A tirade was unleashed against A.Q. Ansari in the press, especially the vernacular press.

The president, in his speech stressed the need for education in the community and called upon the community members to give priority to education. Rayazuddin Ahmad said that education alone will bring prosperity and honour in their lives. He also advised the audience to strengthen 'Momin Gazette' financially which served as the organ of the community in that part of the country. A resolution was later adopted to have a press of its own.

Separate Homeland

Muslim League's movement for a separate homeland had picked up and its claim that the sole representative party of the Indian Muslim was becoming louder. The fact was otherwise. A large number of Ulemas, under the banner of Maulana Hussain Ahmad Madni's Jamiatul Ulema, were entirely against the communal approach of the Muslim League. Moreover, quite a substantial number of Muslim leaders in the length and breadth of the country were within the Congress party. Maulana Abul Kalam Azad, Rafi Ahmad Qidwai, Mohammad Mian, Mufti Atiqur Rahman, Dr. Mokhtar Ahmad Ansari, Dr. Zakir Hussain, Maulana Hifzur Rahman and a score of other leaders formed the top of Congress leadership. Historian Papiya Ghosh writes, "Ansari described the Pakistan scheme as being contrary to 'true' conception of Islam. At the All India Momin Youth Conference, Patna, A.A.M. Noor described the Pakistan scheme as un-Islamic and absolutely impracticable. In November, 1939, A.Q. Ansari as Vice-President of the All India Momin Conference sent telegrams to Gandhi and Rajendra Prasad that four-and-half crore strong Momin community did not accept Muslim League as its representative and wanted separate representation in all matters."

Momin Conference Turns Political

The Gorakhpur resolution brought change in its complexion when it finally decided to enter the electoral arena. It was a smooth transition from a social organisation to a political entity. There was a near consensus in the deliberations on the necessity to counter the danger posed by the Muslim League's demand for a separate homeland for Indian Muslims. While overwhelming majority of the Momin leadership was in favour of its unequivocal support to the Congress party, there were few to be counted, who supported the Muslim League. Momin Conference rose to the political need of the hour.

Shaikh Zahiruddin, Advocate Ambala, was elected the next president of All India Momin Conference. He continued as the national president till he resigned in the year 1948. With its decision to enter the electoral arena, a Momin-Ansar Parliamentary Board was subsequently constituted with Mohiuddin, Bar-at-Law as its first chairman. Elections to the Calcutta Corporation were round the corner and the leadership decided to contest a few seats of the corporation. Barrister Mohiuddin had to plunge in his job of selecting candidates for Calcutta Corporation elections. The decision to contest elections to the Calcutta Corporation was bold and surprising as Calcutta was considered a citadel of Muslim League under the strong leadership of Sir Khawja Nazimuddin, Fazlul Haque Chowdhry, Hussain Shaheed Suhrawardy and Raghib Ahsan. Out of the four Muslim League stalwarts, Raghib Ahsan, from the Ansari community, was considered the strategist of the party. Mohiuddin wrote in his article appearing in '*Ansari Number*' of '*Sada-e-Hind*' Patna (July, 1966) that it was significant to note that while Bengal was under the Muslim League government, two of the Momin Conference candidates: Kalimuddin Chowdhry and Shaikh Basir Ali won the corporation seats by overwhelming majority defeating Muslim League candidates from the assembly constituency of Suhrawardy. When Khawja Nazimuddin was defeated in assembly elections, Muslim League fielded him from the same Patwakhali constituency in a bye election. It was a great set back for Muslim League. The constituency which was considered safe and elected Muslim League stalwarts like H.S. Suhrawardy and Sir Khawja Nazimuddin with overwhelming majorities could be partially encroached upon by Momin Conference, merely a new political outfit. The results of the Calcutta Corporation elections sent shock waves in the Muslim League. It was a moral booster for the Momin Conference and precisely, it was from here that Momin Conference was recognised as a political power.

8th Session of All India Momin Conference, Delhi 1943

The 8th and the last session before independence was held at Delhi on April 26, 27 and 28, 1943 at Aziz Park, near Hardinge library. The national president, Shaikh Zahiruddin, Advocate, Ambala presided over the conference.

This session was held at a time when India was struggling hard to drive out foreign domination and bring Swarajya to the country. Momin Conference had by now recorded its political clout. The Delhi session was held at a time when the entire environment was filled with freedom mission.

In his marathon presidential speech, Momin Conference

President dealt in length the role of the Momin-Ansar community in the freedom movement and its conviction in the secular values of the country. Shaikh Zahiruddin stressed upon the community not to be swayed by communal emotions or considerations that will jeopardize the national interest. He advised the community to be strongly in support of the Indian National Congress at all costs.

(*Further details of the Delhi session could not be available through any source.*)

Momin Conference vs. Muslim League

Abdul Qaiyum Ansari, then the provincial president of Bihar played a significant role in the Calcutta civic elections. He kept shuttling between Patna and Calcutta to monitor the civic elections as a large number of settlers from Bihar formed the electorates. Since Ansari was one of the main architects of transformation of Momin Conference to a political party, he was anxious to see that Momin Conference gets through these elections. A few months after, Ansari organised a massive Momin youth conference at Patna and invited the national president Shaikh Zahiruddin to address. The sequence of events after the historical national session of Momin Conference at Gorakhpur and his strong advocacy to oppose the communal appeal of Muslim League made Abdul Qaiyum Ansari the symbol of nationalism and Hindu-Muslim unity. Within the Momin community throughout the country, Ansari was acceptable as the most promising national leader of their organisation in future.

Rising high on the crest of the unprecedented success of his efforts at the Calcutta civic elections, Ansari as president of the Bihar State Momin Conference, decided to fight assembly elections in Bihar in the year 1946 on the basis of separate electorate. The decision taken in this regard caused embarrassment in the Muslim League circle of Bihar. It was a great challenge for Muslim League since they claimed to be the only party of Muslims and used to brand Congress Muslims as supporter of Hindu Congress. They feared Momin Conference as a formidable electoral rival besides other small Muslim groups. The Muslim League leaders accused Abdul Qaiyum Ansari of misleading the Muslim community. A campaign was unleashed against Ansari and the Momin community through 'Muslim League' mouthpiece in Urdu language 'Manshoor'. The Momin community stood firmly by its unshakable and dynamic leader Abdul Qaiyum Ansari. The volunteers of Muslim League coined a new slogan '*Muslim Hai To Muslim League Mein Aa*' (if you are a Muslim come to the fold of Muslim League) only to damage the prospects of Momin Conference. They used derogatory words against Congress Muslim leaders, leaders of the Momin community and against all those Muslim Ulemas and intellectuals who refused to toe the line of Muslim League. For Momin community, they had favourite satirical poetic line of Akbar Allahabadi—'*Budhu Mian Bhi Hazrat-e Gandhi Kai Saath Hain: Hain Mushte Khaque Magar Andhi Kai Saath Hain*'. Muslim sentiments were aroused by interested quarters against the Momin community and its leaders for alleged jeopardizing the interests of the Muslims.

The author has still a vivid memory of an ugly incident at Patna, the provincial capital of Bihar. The Moradpur area of Patna was the political hub of the Muslim League and the Momin Conference leaders and workers. Everywhere in hotels, shops and streets, the elections were being discussed. The stretch of road between Bankipore post office and Rajendra Surgical ward of the Patna Medical College Hospital was then quite narrow and crowded which was broadened only after independence. Election fever had gripped the state. Slogans and counter slogans in favour of Muslim League and Momin Conference rendered the air as a routine affair. There was a Muslim hotel, Majestic, near Anjuman Islamia Hall on the main road. It was always crowded with mostly a-cup-of-tea customers. All hues of political leaders, Congress, League, Momin Conference, Independent party, etc. routinely gathered round the place, being a market area, make speeches at the Anjuman and then settle in hotels around to discuss politics. One evening it so happened that while some khadi clad Momin leaders and workers, sitting on tables waiting for dinner to be served, a group of Muslim League hoodlums stormed the hotel and snatched dinner plates from them. They hurled abusive language branding them as 'Kafir' and pushed them out of the hotel denying food for them.

The hotel owner was himself quite scared and remained a silent spectator. Almost infront of the Majestic hotel where this incident occurred there was yet another Muslim hotel, just a few steps away, in Do Rukhi Gali running south of the main road owned by Gharibullah who had an emotional attachment with Momin Conference and a staunch supporter of Gandhi. He collected those who were humiliated, brought them to his hotel and served them food. After his death, his son Habibullah became the owner of the hotel and renamed 'Habibia Hotel' which still exists there. The ugly incident was condemned by Congress and Momin leaders. Such ugly scenes were witnessed those days in different places of Bihar.

First State Elections

Undettered by accusations and assault of Muslim League, Momin Conference went ahead and finally set up candidates in 1946 assembly elections as it wanted to establish its political presence by contesting assembly elections through separate electorate and it succeeded in its political mission. The Muslim League had green box and Momin Conference opted for red box, red being symbol of labour. Abdul Qaiyum Ansari, the President of the provincial Momin Conference and by dint of that also Vice-President of All India Momin Conference, was the star campaigner. He was assisted by a strong team of young Momin intellectuals including Md. Yasin Ansari, Hazaribagh; Master Abdur Razaqque Ansari, Jehanabad; Rezaur Rahman Ansari, Advocate, Patna; Abdur Razzaque Ansari, Irba, Ranchi; Md. Yasin Ansari from Santhal Pargana; and Havildar Ansari, Gaya. Subsequently, a large number of Momin personalities from different part of the state, Bengal and United Provinces Punjab, M.P. and Delhi came forward to actively associate with the young, dynamic and flamboyant Momin leadership in Abdul Qaiyum Ansari.

Momin Conference won seven assembly seats. They were, A.Q. Ansari from Ranchi; R.Ali from Plamu; Yasin Ansari, Santhal Pargana; Yasin Ansari, Hazaribag; A.A.Mohammad Noor from Madhubani; Hafiz Manzoor Hussain from Sasaram and Ramzan Ali from Chapaa.

Two Ansaris on Muslim League ticket also won assembly elections. They were Khan Bahadur Mubarak Karim from Biharsharif and Khan Bahadur Latifur Rahman from Gaya. Another M.L. Stalwart, Khan Bahadur Abdul Jalil was trounced by Momin candidate A.A. Md. Noor from Madhubani Mr. Jalil later won to become a member of the legislative assembly. His son Khalilur Rahman was also a MLA.

Coming back to the first assembly elections on the basis of separate electorate in 1937, Maulana Sajjad's Muslim Independent Party (MIP) won 15, Abdul Aziz led Muslim United Party (MUP) 6 and Ahrar 3. In October, 1937 the MUP and the Ahrar merged with the Muslim League. There was some technical hitch for Congress to form a government immediately; therefore the Muslim Independent Party led by Md. Yunus, Barrister, formed an interim ministry between April 1 and July 19, 1937.

Papiya Ghosh gave a description of the short political adjustments of both Muslim Independent Party and Jamiatul Ulema Hind with Muslim League. It says: "Significantly, the MIP decided to cooperate with the Muslim League on December 9, 1937, because it 'too' had declared complete independence as its goal. Six of its members were allowed to join Muslim League. Thus, reducing the strength of MIP in the legislature to nine. Three years later, a resolution of MIP explained that this 'overlapping' arrangement was made at the suggestion of some responsible members of the Muslim League. However, as it turned out the Muslim League had 'always' opposed the MIP within and outside the legislature, and had also passed a resolution that no member of the MIP could join Muslim League. Those who wanted to join Muslim League could resign from MIP."

"By contrast, in neighbouring U.P., the Jamiat Ulema Hind had resigned as a body from the Muslim League Parliamentary Board on Maulana Azad's persuasion in 1937."

The research made by Papiya Ghosh on pre-independence Muslim politics, especially in Bihar and put in her latest book before her assassination, clearly indicates that both MIP and Jamiat Ulema Hind had short political honeymooning with Muslim League, on one basis or another, but it is equally a historical fact that at no point of time Momin Conference had ever collaborated with Muslim League on any account.

Papiya Ghosh further wrote— "On the eve of the 1946 elections to the state assemblies based on separate electorate when Dr. Rajendra Prasad was worried over the fate of the 40 Muslim seats of the provincial legislature, he noted that of the Congress Muslims, the Muslim Independent Party and Jamiat-al. Ulema-i-Hind and the Momins, the only active body was Momin Conference.

Ultimately, the Jamiat contested 9, the Congress 10 and Momin Conference 20 seats. The Muslim League swept 34, the Congress 1, the Jamiat got none and Momin Conference 6 seats. The Muslim League candidates were defeated by Momin Conference by a margin of 254 to 1095 votes. Since Ansari had won on Momin conference ticket; he had initial hurdles in being inducted to Dr. Sri Krishna's cabinet. Ansari refused to sign Congress pledge as a moral gesture. Subsequently on intervention of Sardar Patel, Ansari was inducted as a cabinet minister with P.W.D. and Cottage Industries departments without fulfilling the obligation of formally signing the party pledge. The Muslim Independent party which had bagged 15 state legislature seats in 1937 elections went blank due to the death of its founder Maulana Sajjad in 1940.

With its decision to contest assembly elections and encouraging results achieved, Momin Conference had infused new life in the Momin community. There was a wave of excitement in the community who had been lying low for centuries.

In the United Provinces, Momin leaders including Reyazuddin Ahmad, Advocate and Nezamuddin, Advocate, Allahabad; Sheikh Murtaza Hussain and his son Istefa Hussain, Gorakhpur; Hakim Hazique, Itawa; Zahoor Bhaijan and Abdul Qadeer, Moradabad were deeply involved in the movement. Hafiz Abdul Aziz Abdul Latif, Dhulia and Sayeed Sheikh Engineer, Bombay; Abu Shams Abdul Ghafoor, Shamsuddin, Engineer, Maulana Md. Yahya from Calcutta; Md. Ibrahim Ansari, Hydrabad; Hafiz Manzoor Hussain, Arrah, Sardar Islam and his son, Sardar Latifur Rahman, Gaya; Khan Bahadur Abdul Jalil, Advocate, Darbhanga; Khan Bahadur Mobarak Karim, Biharsharif; Maulvi Saminuddin, Bhagalpur; Abdus Sami Nadvi, Darbhanga; Master Alijan Ansari, Purnia and Hakim Muniruddin, and Md. Salim Ansari advocate Bhagalpur; Ibrahim Ansari, M.P.; R.Ali, MLA; and Zahoor Ali, Ranchi; Asim Bihari, Biharsharif besides Maula Bux Thekadar, Hakim Ajmali and Hafiz Abdul Aziz, Delhi were in the forefront of the movement. The social and political movement that Ansari spearheaded got unequivocal support from every section of the community. While Momin leaders in Muslim League had reservations about Ansari's political ideology, but they were fully in his support of his social mission. They included Raghib Ahsan, Khan Bahadur Abdul Jalil, Darbhanga; Khan Bahadur Mobarak Karim, Biharsharif; and Raees Nagmatia, Sardar Latifur Rahman.

A.Q. Ansari and A.A.M. Noor

Though literally, Momin Conference was born in the city of Calcutta only by the collective efforts of Momin leaders from Bihar, it grew up in the state of Bihar. It came into national prominence only after it turned political and scored amazingly in its maiden elections of Calcutta Corporation. The Congress party found a numerically strong Muslim ally in its struggle for freedom.

Abdul Qaiyum Ansari, deeply involved in his political mission, found another young and dynamic personality with the same zeal and spirit from the land of Purnia in North Bihar. He was Abul Ahad Mohammad Noor, well built, tall with a very impressive personality. With his dedication to the cause of the most depressed Momin-Ansari community, he proved himself as the person second-in-command in the state Momin politics. Both Momin leaders together, created political waves, rose to great heights and had full command over Bihar politics. They earned respect and popularity and left indelible mark on Bihar politics.

These leaders of the Momin-Ansar community in Bihar, Abdul Qaiyum Ansari and Abul Ahad Mohammad Noor presented a united leadership with a strong following of young team of highly educated youngsters around them, always ready to provide services to the two leaders spearheading the movement. A.Q. Ansari and A.A.M. Noor showed their utmost patience to bear the onslaught of a section of Muslims belonging to Muslim League camp and even of those in the Congress party with narrow caste prejudice. These leaders had many twists and tribulations in their lives to reach the top of political power in the state. Unmindful of their opponents within the Muslim community's narrow caste-based outlook, Ansari and Noor went ahead with the noble mission to wipe out the shame of un-Islamic practice of caste system from the Indian Muslim society with strong determination. Paucity of fund never came in their way. During early days of the movement, a friend of mine who resided in Alamgunj Mohalla of old Patna, Dr. Akhtar Alam gave me full account of their style of working and living. Besides Dr. Alam, other young boys of his age group were very much impressed with the zeal with which the Momin leaders were spearheading the movement. This made the young men attracted with a sense to serve and cooperate with these leaders. In course of time, there was an army of young men around who were always ready to march ahead in their leader's footsteps.

Among them was one Rezaur Rahman Ansari, most intelligent and dynamic. It is said that he was the first person of the Momin community of Alamgunj who graduated. In fact, though the community in the area was economically well off since there were a number of big businessmen and traders in the Mohallah including the house of Noorani Bagh, but education eluded them. When the news about Rezaur Rahman Ansari spread, there was jubilation in the local Momins and he was taken out in procession of elephants. Later, he did law and practiced in the local court.

On the main road of the Alamgunj area of Patna city area thickly populated with the community, there was a Momin building, on the first floor of which the two Momin leaders used to stay while in Patna. They had only one room at their disposal that served both as bed room and office room for the leaders. A.Q. Ansari always carried a small bed roll wrapped in a Duree and a Badhna or Lota hanging from the string of the bed roll and a small box. Though coming from an aristocratic family, Ansari's simplicity and his punctuality in offering Namaz, five times without any default, very much impressed everybody that added to his popularity. He had great impact on his life of his maternal grandfather, Maulana Abdullah Ghazipuri who was an Islamic scholar of repute of Wahabi school of Islamic thought. His mother was a very religious and pious lady.

There was a distinct contrast in personalities of the two top most Momin leaders of Bihar, both in temperament and way of dealing. Both these leaders of the Momin community had exceptional human qualities in different form.

Abdul Qaiyum Ansari belonged to an affluent family. He was the son of Munshi Abdul Haque Ansari a contractor of Dehri-on-Sone. He originally belonged to village Neoli in Ghazipore district of U.P. His father shifted to Dehri in the nineteenth century. He was soft spoken; highly cultured. Fair complexioned, a bit hefty sharp features of above average height commanded a pleasing personality. Anybody who ever met Ansari found mismerised with his simplicity and cultured behaviour. He was the most popular and highly respected leader of Bihar. His political career began during the Khilafat and non-cooperation movements. Ansari was the secretary of the Shahabad District Congress Committee between 1930 and 1931. A.Q. Ansari, eldest of three brothers, used to go to school in Sasaram from Dehri-on-Sone along with his elder brother in a private pheaton. After school education, he first studied at Aligarh and then moved to Calcutta. Khilafat movement made a great impact on the life and style of Ansari. Till the time he was influenced by Khilafat Movement spearheaded by Maulna Jauhar Ali and Maulana Md. Ali, his living was lavish and stylish. Once he entered politics, he gave up everything worth style its name and sported Khadi or handloom Kurta and Pyjama and a simple pair of sleepers occasionally wearing Achkan to lead a simple life. For all these qualities, A.Q. Ansari commanded great respect in the party and Congress leadership from Nehru to Indira who had great appreciation for him. Once it so happened that Shambhu Nath Jha, news editor of Searchlight, Patna (now ceased publication) rang up Ansari and wanted to talk to him. That moment I was alone in the room so I picked up the receiver to respond to his call. I noticed that Jhaji was a bit emotional and in a hurry to talk to Ansari. I told him that he was in the bath room but assured him that as soon as he comes out he would talk to him. A few minutes after Ansari came, Shambhu Nath Jha told Ansari that he was having Delhi edition of "Statesman" in his hand which has given a lead story about the probable names for nomination as the Vice-President of India. Quoting insiders, the correspondent wrote that two probable names of Justice Hydatullah and Abdul Qaiyum Ansari of Bihar were being discussed by the Congress High Command. As is known, decision went in favour of Justice Hidayatullah. Ansari became a cabinet minister as early as in 1946 in Dr. Sri Krishna Sinha's first cabinet and died in harness in 1973 while he was a cabinet minister of the government headed by Kedar Pandey, a leader quite junior to him. He rose to great heights. Ansari became President of Bihar Congress and a Member of Rajya Sabha. Though literally, he was a Bihar leader but in stature he was the tallest and nobody, especially amongst Congress Muslims, could measure upto him in sacrifice and unparallel contribution to the party and the country. He was a strong pillar of secularism and nationalism. He never compromised with communal outlook. He had a clean public life. It was his sheer ill luck that he could not find a berth in Union Cabinet and his candidature for leadership of the State Congress Legislature Party was also frustrated at the eleventh hour. At every stage of his life till death, he maintained utmost simplicity. Ansari, in his lifetime, became a legendry figure of the Momin movement.

Ansari adorned a number of high political positions. He was one of the eleven members of the 1955 Kalelkar Backward Classes Commission and President of the All India Backward Muslim Federation in 1952.

Another towering personality of the Momin community in Bihar, Abul Ahad Mohammad Noor came from a lower middle class family of a handloom weaver in Purnia. He was born in Madhepur in Madhubani district in his maternal house. He got his early education and brought up in Madhepur. Later, he shifted to Purnia where he practiced as a Mokhtar in the lower court. In the later part of his life he built his own house in Maulvi Tola of Purnia town. The characteristic of Noor's personality was that since his early life he was known as an outspoken and straight forward person. At the seventh annual session of All India Momin Conference at Gorakhpur in 1939, A.A.M. Noor who was already elected M.L.C. of Bihar Legislative Council, moved a resolution that the future constitution of the country should be framed by a constituent assembly based on adult franchise with a separate electorate for Momins. The demand was made on the ground that the electoral roll prepared on the basis of present franchisee rested on property, tax paying and educational qualifications and protected the interest of the so-called upper caste Muslims represented by the Muslim League. Thus, the present system of franchisee was against the basic norms of democracy.

A.A.M. Noor had to struggle hard to find a place of honour in politics. He was a man of clear vision that made him to climb to great heights. Since Md. Noor was brought up in the surrounding of weavers, he knew their agony and distress very well. It was this feeling that once in power; he dedicated himself to the task of economic emancipation and welfare of the handloom weavers of the state. With the unequivocal support of A.Q. Ansari, he was instrumental in organising the handloom weavers of the state through co-operative societies affiliated to an apex organisation at the state level. With these two leaders of the weaver community in the saddle of power and in tune with the government's policy, the traditional handloom industry in the state once again flourished after a long set back during the British Raj. The apex co-operative body of the state, The Bihar State Handloom Weavers Co-operative Union Ltd. purchased a piece of land to construct an exclusive building in its own name in the peripheral area of Patna known as

Rajendra Nagar. But somehow or another, the proposed building could not become a reality in their lifetime.

Maulana Abul Mohasin Mohammad Sajjad, the founder of Imarat Shariah, Bihar and Orissa, formed Muslim Independent party. In 1937, during separate electorate, it fielded its candidates to win maximum Muslim seats in the assembly elections. In view of the then prevailing situation, Maulana Sajjad wanted to select persons commanding good oratory who could effectively place the viewpoint of the community in the legislative council. Md. Noor had impressed Maulana with his views in a number of meetings of Jamiatul Ulema and Imarat Shariah. Finally, Noor was nominated to become M.L.C. in 1938 by the Muslim Independent party.

This was his first entry to state legislature. Md. Noor contested first assembly elections in 1946 on separate electorate from Madhubani constituency and trounced his Muslim League rival Khan Bahadur Abdul Jalil, a prominent advocate of Darbhanga also from the Momin community. He was made Parliamentary Secretary, Education and Public Relations in Dr. Sri Krishna Sinha's cabinet with A.Q. Ansari at the cabinet level.

It is significant to note that Md. Noor was allotted No. 1, Sepentine Road as his official residence when he became Parliamentary Secretary in the first cabinet after independence. He preferred to continue to occupy the same bungalow even after he was elevated as Dy. Minister and Minister of State and lived there till his death. He died at Patna on October 11, 1974. For almost three decades, he occupied the bungalow, a sort of record in itself. All through this long period, Noor was a member of the House uninterrupted and when he died, he remained a member of Bihar Legislative Council. A.A. Md. Noor was a man of high intellect and a shrewd politician. He was known in the Congress circle as a political forecaster. His closest political friend, Deo Shran Singh, Daroga Prasad Roy who later became Chief Minister, Ram Lakhan Singh Yadav and scores of other leaders banked heavily on his forecast. Once during a keen contest of state congress legislature party's leader election, A.A.M. Noor was spotted in Binodanand Jha's camp. That was enough indication that Jha was going to be elected the leader of the state legislature party. Every congressman was so sure and even the newspapers safely forecasted his success and it really happened.

Communal riots of 1946 took a very serious turn and South Bihar was badly affected. Hundreds of Muslims were massacred and thrown in village wells. President of the All India Momin Conference, Shaikh Zahiruddin decided to visit riot torn areas of Bihar. He came from Ambala and stayed with Abul Ahad Md. Noor at 1, Serpentine road. Md. Noor's son Khalid Rashid Saba and I had an opportunity to be close to him during his stay. He was extra ordinary tall and had a very impressive personality. He loved children. In the evening, when both of us used to play cricket at the back yard, Shaikh Zahiruddin would come to us and just enjoy playing cricket with us.

Shaikh Zahiruddin in company with cabinet minister Abdul Qaiyum Ansari who also happened to be state president of Momin Conference and parliamentary secretary Abul Ahad Md. Noor toured the badly affected riot hit areas. He was shocked and outraged to hear the barbarism of the perpetrators of riots. He was completely broken. More shocking was the fact that those perished in the riots were mostly from the lower strata of the Muslim society, those who were the torch bearer of Hindu-Muslim unity and those who dared to oppose Muslim League's demand for a separate homeland for Muslims. The Momin Conference national president came heavily on Dr. Sri Krishna Sinha government for its failure to save the lives of the innocent population of the state. He took it as betrayal of Muslims by his government. Immediately after his return, he sent his resignation from the presidentship of the Momin Conference and left for Karachi in sheer disgust.

Shaikh Zahiruddin's resignation was a drawback for the Momin movement. Abdul Qaiyum Ansari had by now acquired popularity among the Ansari community all over the country. All eyes turned towards Ansari. He became the unanimous choice for leading the movement. Even Momin leaders of Muslim League faction did not oppose Ansari's candidature and silently supported him.

The working committee of the All India Momin Conference was held at Patna. Abdul Qaiyum Ansari was elected next president of All India Momin Conference unanimously. The working committee members expressed their confidence in Ansari's leadership.

9th Session of All India Momin Conference, Patna, 1948

After taking full command of the Momin movement at the national level, Ansari held the 9th session in Patna at Bankipore Lawn, now Gandhi Maidan on March 26, 27 and 29, 1948. This session was held precisely six years after the 8th session in Delhi.

Patna session assumed significance as it was the first session after independence. The political atmosphere had totally changed. Hard days of struggle were over for the community and its leaders were in an upbeat mood. Momin Conference was riding on the crest of unprecedented victory. There was a sense of victory over the obscurantist and bigoted elements of the Muslim community, apparently visible from their faces, and a sense of political satisfaction was also evident to the effect that ultimately their political ideology prevailed and became successful. It was in this background that the Patna session was held. Ansari was the leading figure. During that period, I was a class IX student and so I have a vivid memory of the entire show. Momin leaders from outside the state attended the session. Besides the working committee members, a large contingent from West Bengal and Uttar Pradesh came down to Patna. Almost all the founders of the Momin movement from Bengal, Delhi and U.P. attended Patna session. Enthusiasm and excitement invaded the Momin- Ansari community of the state who made a bee line to the state capital. It resembled like a festive occasion. It was Momin Conference everywhere. People from every part of the state were continuously pouring in since morning.

A city of tents sprang up at the sprawling Bankipore Lawn. Momin Conference flags were fluttering on strategic places in the town. The spacious Pandal and the entire area of the session were decorated with buntings and festoons. Tastefully decorated gates named after leaders of the Momin movement were erected that added colour to the occasion. "Ansar Scouts" from Moradabad played the welcome band and presented guard of honour to the incoming president. The deliberations of the momentous occasion were filmed by the state government that is still lying in the archives of the Public Relations Department. Daronacharya, the legendry photographer of Bihar had shown his skill in filming the historic occasion.

Prominent Congress leaders were vying with each other to have a prominent place on the dais to record their presence on this momentous occasion. Abdul Qaiyum Ansari was a cabinet minister. He was allotted departments of P.W.D and Relief and Rehabilitation. Another Momin leader Abul Ahad Md. Noor was the Parliamentary Secretary. Besides more than half a dozen Momin legislators of the state and those from U.P., Momin ministers from the neighbouring state were also present on the dais.

The session began with recitation from the holy Quran. Ansari made a very emotional speech and paid tributes to the Momin-Ansar community who stood firmly with the Indian National Congress braving all sorts of adverse situations.

Patna session was held at the back drop of assassination of Gandhi. Ansari made a frontal attack on the fascist communal elements which had orphaned the nation and cautioned to be on guard against such elements. A.Q. Ansari paid glowing tribute to Mahatma Gandhi and said that without any arm struggle India could attain independence, that is unique in itself and the whole world admired Gandhi for his non-violence.

Ansari reminded the Momin community of the role played by the Momin Conference in the last twenty years of its existence and said that it played a positive role in fighting out caste prejudices prevalent in the Muslim society that gave moral courage and a sense of belonging to the most depressed class among the Muslims. He was generous in his praise of those who founded the movement. A.Q. Ansari in his impassionate speech dealt in length about the role played by the Momin Conference as a political entity and said that it will go down in the history for its unparallel role in the freedom movement and for strengthening the integrity of the nation. Making an oblique reference to 'Muslim League Friends', Ansari regretted their shameful behaviour towards the Momin community members as they had to face unspeakable humiliation and ordeals at their hands. However, he said that since now India was a free nation and these friends feel highly demoralized and ashamed of their role, one feels pity towards them and, therefore, should be treated with the attitude of forgive and forget.

In the concluding portion of his presidential speech, Abdul Qaiyum Ansari told the conference that during the last session of Momin conference at Gorakhpur, it had become imperative to declare Momin Conference a political entity to fight out against communal approach of muslim league. Momin Conference successfully accomplished its role and is genuinely proud of its historical decision. Since now the political scenario is changed and India was a sovereign nation, presence of a separate political body of the Momin community does not seem to be justified. In the same breath, Ansari put proposal that the community should henceforth join the Indian National Congress enblock as hopefully, Congress will take care of its political aspirations. His proposal was echoed with intensive clappings from the huge crowd and slogans of 'Momin Conference Zindabad' and 'Congress Zindabad', putting a lid over the political functions of their body.

The Chief Minister, Dr. Sri Krishna Sinha, overwhelmed by the grand success of the conference and presence of the top leaders of the All India Momin Conference from different parts of the country at the dais, complimented the Momin community and the sagacious leadership of A.Q. Ansari for playing a very difficult and positive role in the national struggle for freedom. Dr. Sinha said that the Momin community of India had scripted history of which India was proud of.

Other prominent persons who spoke on the occasion included Ansari leader and Parliamentary Secretary A.A.M. Noor, guest Ansari leaders from other states and Congress leaders.

A poem on the assassination of Gandhi was read that touched the hearts of the people. Since his murder was a recent episode, people became emotional and a number of leaders on the dias were noticed wiping tears. The theme of the poem was:

> *"Jagao Na Bapu Ko Neend Aa gaee Hai; Ahimsa Tashaddud Sai Takra Gai Hai"*
> (Do not wake up bapu, he is in deep slumber:
> Non-violence had come to collision with violence.)

Abdul Qaiyum Ansari reconstituted his working committee, which was as follows:

> *President:* Abdul Qaiyum Ansari; *General Secretary:* A.A. Shaikh, B.E.; *Jt. Secretaries:* Hakim Bashir Ahmad and Hafiz Manzoor Husain; *Assistant Secretary:* Md. Abdur Razzaque, B.A.(Hons); *Tresurer:* Qari Abdul Latif; *Observers:* Hakim Hazique and Babu Md. Hussain

> **Working Committee:** West Bengal: Professor Md. Senaullah, Md. Shamsuddin Ahmad, Maulana Md. Yahya, Dr. Qutbunuddin Ahmad, Abdul Matin; Bihar: Rezaur Rahman Ansari, B.A. (Hons), Md. Yasin Ansari, M.L.A. (Hazaribagh), Maulvi Asim Bihari, Abdus Salim, B.A., B.L, Md. Ibrahim Ansari, B.A., B.L.; C.P. and Berar : Haji Abdul Qadir, Saith Md. Qasim Letafat, Saith Kalimullah; U.P.: Reyazuddin Ahmad, B.A., L.L.B; Nezamuddin, B.A., L.L.B; Babu.Md. Hassan; Hakim Hazique; Soofi Abdul Wahid; Istefa Hussain, Advocate; Dr. Md. Abdur Razzaque Ansari; Bombay: Haji Abdur Razzaque, Malegaon; Delhil and East Punjab: Maulana Md. Usman, Maulana Hafeezuddin; Assam: Mohiuddin, Bar-at-law.

Leadership of the Momin Conference had travelled from Punjab to Bihar for the first time. It was now in the command of Abdul Qaiyum Ansari who had by now acquired an important position in the national political arena because of his unflinching support to the Indian National Congress and his firm stand against communal politics.

The first meeting of the reorganised working committee of the All India Momin Conference met at Hameed Manzil Allahabad on December 24, at 3:30 p.m.under the chairmanship of Abdul Qaiyum Ansari, its president. It deliberated for four hours and adjourned at 7:30 p.m. It again met next day (December 25) at 9 a.m. The following members attended the working committee meeting:

> *President*: Abdul Qaiyum Ansari; *General Secretary*: A.A. Shaikh (Bombay); *Jt. Secretary*: Ali Hassan Asim Bihari; Dr. Abdur Razaqque, Allahabad; Reyazur Rahman, Advocate, Allahabad; Hakim Bashir Ahmad Moradabadi; *Jt. Secretary*: Hakim Hazique, Itawah (U.P.); Md. Yasin Ansari, M.L.A., Hazaribagh; Hafiz Manzoor Hussain, M.L.A., Bihar; Haji Abdul Latif, Moradabad *Treasurer*; Maulvi Abdur Razzaque, Malegaon; Istefa Hussain, Advocate, Gorakhpur; Ibrahim Ansari, Ranchi; Md. Abdur Razzaque Ansari, Bihar, Abdul Matin, B.A, Calcutta, Abdur Razzaque Ansari, Bombay- Secretary, A.I.M.C.

The working committee recalled the resolution of Patna session held in March last, which decided to dissociate itself from political activities and go back to its original form of a social and economic organization. It confirmed the decision. In another related resolution, it called upon the Momin-Ansar community to join Congress in the larger interest of the community and the country.

The working committee constituted following sub-committees:

Organisation Sub-committee: consisting of the *President* and the *General Secretary*, Maulvi Nezamuddin (U.P.), M.A. Razzaque (Bihar) and M. Haneef Khumar (Bombay).

Programme Sub-committee: consisting of the *President* and *General Secretary*, Hakim Bashir Ahmad, Istefa Hussain (U.P.), Haji Abdul Qadeer (C.P), M.A.Matin (West Bengal) and Reyazuddin Ahmad (Allahabad).

Yarn Sub-committee: consisting of A.A. Shaikh, *Convenor*, M. Haneef Khumar, Munnu Mian Latafat, Seth Abdur Razzaque, Seth Haji Abdus Samad, Y.M. Panoniker and Hakim Bashir Ahmad.

Handloom Industry Planning Committee: consisting of Abdul Qaiyum Ansari, *Chairman*; A.A. Shaikh, *Secretary*; Hakim Bashiur Ahmad, Abdul Hai Mahavi (Assistant Registrar, Cooperative Societies, Bombay Government); Md. Yasin, Deputy Director of Cottage Industries, Government of Bihar; S. Haneef Khumar, Maulvi Nezamuddin, Maulvi Asim Bihari and Abdur Razzaque Ansari, Bihar.

Resolutions passed at the first meeting of the working committee of A.I.M.C. held at Allahabad:

1. It was decided to establish Momin Chamber of Commerce with its branches in important cities.
2. Through another resolution, the W.C. decided to raise a fund of rupees one lakh for the A.I.M.C.

It was decided that the next meeting of the W.C. will be held at Bombay in February, next.

A very embracing situation was faced in the first meeting of the working committee. Before the election of Abdul Qaiyum Ansari as the national president, the two stalwarts of the Momin Conference in Bihar viz. Ansari and Noor pulled together in a very cordial atmosphere. There was excellent understanding between the two leaders. During the meeting of the first Working Committee, it was brought to the notice of the leadership that A.A. Md. Noor, who headed state Momin Conference after the elevation of A.Q. Ansari to the national level, had issued a statement appearing in leading newspapers of Patna of October 21, 1948 including 'Indian Nation', 'Searchlight' and as the resolution put it, in Urdu 'Momin Duniya,' known to be an organ of Noor Saheb, that the state unit was a totally independent unit and All India Momin Conference has no constitutional control over it. Moreover, it is alleged that Md. Noor also castigated the national leadership and described the All India body as a defunct body. The statement of Md. Noor was taken seriously. The Working Committee expressed its deep anguish over Noor's press statement and termed it completely unacceptable. Mr. Noor was charged with anti-organisation activity. Through a resolution, Noor was expelled from the primary membership of Momin Conference. The resolution was moved by Md. Nezamuddin, Advocate from Allahabad and seconded by Abdul Matin, Bengal. What made Md. Noor to issue such a statement castigating Ansari could not be known. Anyhow, when the dust settled down, Ansari withdrew suspension and the situation eased. Further details about this unpleasant episode could not be found through any of the papers available in the file which was handed over to the author by Sayeed Shaikh Engineer, general secretary when this author met him in Bombay. But through another resolution, the state Momin Conference of West Bengal was granted 'temporary affiliation' conditionally. It shows that under its constitution, state units were granted affiliation temporarily on certain conditions. What were these conditions is not clear.

It is worth noting that both these Momin leaders, Ansari and Noor had tremendous respect and regard for each other. It was an unusual phenomenon in political lives. As is so common in politics, on both sides there were certain elements who on minutest provocation would try to fan differences and create condition for confrontation. Sometimes it might be during elections to the state apex handloom cooperative body, being considered the hub of Momin politics or holding of state level or district level Momin conference, these elements were always ready to create misunderstanding between these top leaders. In this particular case also, both refused to listen to their respective supporters and very soon, they forgot the bitterness created and met in a most cordial atmosphere. Once during the elections to the apex Handloom Cooperative Union at Patna, either group had drawn swords and the atmosphere was highly tense. Outside elements were always ready to exploit the situation. On this score, the '*Sangam*' Urdu daily of Patna, owned and edited by a prominent person from another backward caste of Muslim community took lead and spared no efforts to create bitterness between Ansari and Noor. On the day of election, the paper came out with its lead story regarding the elections which was woven in a manner as if heaven was going to fall and these two Momin leaders, who till now dominated the politics of the state, will lay apart. But all such elements were highly frustrated and had to bite dust. Ansari group won the elections and showed his greatness that he went to meet Noor at his residence. This fully diffused the week long tension, created unnecessarily. Next moment, there was no sign of any difference between the two leaders.

On another such occasion, both Ansari and Noor were at loggerheads on one or another organisational issue. Interested quarters both inside and outside of the Momin community had a good opportunity to play up the situation. The situation was causing concern to the entire Momin community.

Ansari was then the Health Minister of the state. One day while he was on an official tour in his car, he was hit on his arm with the York of a bullock cart passing by his vehicle, causing fracture. He was admitted to the Patna Medical College Hospital where he stayed for a long period. One day it so happened that while I was going back to my residence after finishing my work in the press, as usual I stopped for a while to talk to Ansari Saheb. He was in a pensive mood. I asked him why he was so calm and a bit morosed. He then broke his silence and said that it is my suggestion that you should come out with an editorial expressing a bit of genuine concern on our estranged relation and suggest that as the entire community was suffering, both Ansari and Noor should patch up their differences, if any, in the larger interest of the community. I was rather amazed to hear his reconciling words as the same morning he was so bitter against Noor on certain issues. I tried to gather strength to make some query on that score but he was not ready to listen. He continued and with a flash in his eyes asked me abruptly—"What do you think, if I ring him now, will he not respond positively and come down to meet me here?" Deeply amused over his sudden change of heart, I could with great difficulty say 'yes, certainly so'.

At home, I started weaving a suitable editorial as suggested by Ansari Saheb. Next morning, I went a bit earlier so that I could show the write up to him before going to the press. It was exactly 10.30 in the morning when I reached VIP ward of the Rajendra Surgical block of Patna Medical College Hospital. As I was parking my Lambretta scooter, it was rather amazing to find the car of Noor Saheb parked in the portico. Next moment, I could realize everything. Ansari had not the patience to wait for my editorial and instead, might have rung up Noor Saheb who immediately reciprocated. Time and again, whenever efforts were made to bring about misunderstanding between the two Momin leaders, from within or outside, with a very great sense of responsibility, they will loose no time to patch up and create congenial atmosphere for the sake of entire Momin community.

In any organisation, more so in political ones, when it becomes viable and strong, grouping is bound to crop up. It happened with Momin Conference also. In Bihar, there were clearly two groups of prominent Momin leaders who showed their allegiance with their respective leaders, Ansari and Noor. Since Abul Ahad Md. Noor came from Purnia, most of the leaders of North Bihar always expressed their solidarity with Noor Saheb. They included Maulvi Sami Nadvi from Darbhanga, Shafiqullah Ansari from Madhubani, Alijan Ansari from Baisee and others. However, prominent leaders from North, Hafiz Idris Ansari from Dhaka, Champaran; Ali Sher Ansari, from Sitamarhi; and Haji Tabarak Hussain Ansari were staunch supporters of A.Q. Ansari as he had relatively larger followings. Hafiz Manzoor Hussain from Arrah, Abdur Razzaque Ansari from Irba and R.Ali, Zahoor Ali from Ranchi, Yasin Ansari from Hazaribagh, Master Abdur Razzaque Ansari from Patna, Yasin Ansari of Mudhupur popularly known in Momin circles as Santhali Yasin to differentiate him from Yasin Ansari of Hazaribagh, Ghulam Rasool Ansari and Bashir Ahmad Ansari, Advocate and Israel Ansari, of Collapsable Gate, Dhanbad, Dr. Matiullah and Salim Ansari of Gaya are a few names besides a large number of Momin leaders of South Bihar who stood strongly with Ansari Saheb. However, Maulvi Saminuddin from Bhagalpur, a very dignified Momin leader of Bihar who became Member of Parliament hated groupism within the Momin leadership. He had great respect for both A.Q. Ansari and Abul Ahmad Md. Noor. Despite the allegiance of state Momin leaders to Ansari and Noor, it was significant to note that, irrespective of this allegiance, they had tremendous amount of respect and regard for both of these top leaders.

However, all through long period of its existence, both as a social organization and a political entity, Momin Conference remained a strong united organization. Certainly with two apparent groups in Bihar, the citadel of the movement, were seen but that did never escalate into dissidence. In the neighbouring state of Uttar Pradesh, the same situation existed. Though, Maulvi Habibur Rahman Nomai had his own small group but he always expressed his allegiance to the undisputed leadership of Z.R. Ansari. Maulvi Nomani was once even suspended from the organization for anti-organisation activity for a short period, but Nomani never thought for any parallel Momin organization.

Ansari and Noor were the senior most leaders of the Momin Conference and both commanded respect and regard amongst Momins of the state. Ansari was the most sought after national leader and had become a legendry figure in his life time for his community. In Congress hierarchy, Ansari was on the top. I had on several occasions the opportunity to accompany him to Delhi, Lucknow, Bombay, Bhadohi, Allahabad, Kanpur and a number of other places for organizational engagements. I have yet to find a leader of his popularity whether in power or out of power. Three decades after his death, Ansaris living in rural or urban areas all over the country still remember him with respect. He was a leader who ruled over the hearts of the people. He was a soft spoken, extremely gentle, highly religious person. He was so humble that he never allowed even his Chaprasi to tighten the belts of his bed roll in preparation of a tour. When out of power, even for a short period, he would prefer to move on rickshaw. He had no vehicle of his own as he could not afford one. He could not even purchase a plot of land for his house.

With national leadership of the Momin Conference coming to Bihar, all activities centered round Abdul Qaiyum Ansari. Bihar had played a significant role in organizing the Momin movement. Now that the Congress party was in power in the state with two Ansari leaders in the cabinet and half a dozen Ansari M.L.As in the state legislature, the community was all set to reap the political harvest. The entire community was in an upbeat mood. On the other side, the humiliating defeat of the ideology of the Muslim League and the division of the country created a deep sense of guilt among the Muslim League leaders and supporters of the communal body. Apart from these M.L. leaders, even a section of Congress Muslim leaders who always suffered from caste prejudices, were not happy with the position Momin community as a whole and in particular, Ansari leaders were enjoying after independence.

The Momin leaders never compromised with communal ideology and were strong pillars of secularism. Their actions and every public statement reflected these ideals which were never appreciated by those elements. They were nursing enmity in their hearts against Momin leaders.

In Bihar, in the early stage of the Momin movement, there were a number of Momin leaders and activists who contributed richly to strengthen this movement. In the district of Ranchi, one Haji Abdullah Sardar alias Bega Mian, was the wealthiest person of the entire area in those days. A story goes to suggests that once when forefather of Maharajah Chotanagpur was in need of financial help temporarily, Bega Mian offered the required loan measured in a 'Katora' (a ball for the measurement of rice). The Maharaja reciprocated the gesture of Bega Mia by conferring Tam Patra to the Momin leader. In the year 1922 in Sarna Momin Conference, he was conferred 'Sardari' of twelve villages, a greal public honour. Though he was an illiterate person but was a philanthropist. In Ranchi, another prominent person of the Momin community was R. Ali. He was an influential person of the community. Yet another important person was Shaikh Imamuddin, Advocate who was born in Itki, Ranchi. First Member of Parliament from Bihar after independence was Md. Ibrahim Ansari.

In the district of Champaran, several names require to be mentioned. They were Hafiz Deen Mohammad Ansari (1881-1947), Hafiz Tabarak Hussain (1891-1985), Md. Sayeed Ansari, Hussain Mian Ansari, Abdul Ghani Ansari, Pir Md. Monis, son of Thangal Mian Ansari (1893-1947). In the later years, Md. Sharfuddin Ahmad Qadri of Bettiah and Abdul Hameed Ansari, arms dealer, were active in the Momin Conference. In Sitamarhi, Maulana Abdur Rashid, Diljan Ansari, and Ali Sher Ansari were actively associated with the movement. Pir Mohammad Ansari was a member of the Bihar Legislative Assembly. In the district of Muzaffarpur in the early days of the movement were Maqsood Ali, Abdul Hameed Ansari whose house was torched by British army, Abdus Shakoor Ansari and Shahadat Hussain Jigar Mehsavi of Mehsi, played active role as freedom fighters and were also Momin Conference activists. In Purnia, besides Alijan Ansari who became a member of the state assembly after independence, Shrafat Ali Ansari was the strong pillars of the movement. In the district of Gaya, the House of Nagmatia was a strong centre of the movement as both Sardar Islam and son Sardar Latifur Rahman were dedicated to the Momin movement. Sardar Md. Islam, who was Honarary Magistrate, was credited for creating a strong base for the movement in Bihar in its early days. Other notable persons of Gaya in the movement were Maulana Abdul Karim, Havildar Ansari, Dr. Matiullah of Karim Gunj and Md. Salim Ansari, prominent yarn merchant of Bihar.

Abdur Razzaque Ansari

A weaver revolutionary, an educationist and a politician from the land of Chotanagpur. A.Q. Ansari's most trusted person, Abdur Razzaque Ansari hailed from Irba village near Ranchi. Basically, he was a handloom weaver but being an educationist too, both he and his wife took care of educational upliftment of the downtrodden Momin-Ansar community of the area which was once educationally quite backward. He strongly believed that rampant illiteracy amongst the community was the road block to their development and progress as well as, the root cause of social backwardness. He gave priority to education and established middle school in the name of his leader, Abdul Qaiyum Ansari at Irba. He was mainly instrumental in bringing educational revolution in the tiny hamlet of Irba.

Abdur Razzaque Ansari was highly enterprising person. He spearheaded cooperative movement in the handloom sector of the state. He made personal efforts to form Handloom Cooperative Societies in Chotanagpur area that brought prosperity to the handloom weavers. These societies were affiliated to the Apex Handloom Cooperative Union at Patna. Later, Chotanagpur Regional Cooperative Union was the most viable of all the regional unions in both Bihar and Jharkhand, taken together.

A.R. Ansari had to struggle hard to reach the top position of Chairman of the most prestigious handloom cooperative body. In recognition of his great services to the handloom cooperative movement, he was nominated one of the directors of All India Handloom Fabrics Cooperative Society; which runs Handloom Houses across the country, as a representative of his viable handloom body.

Abdur Razzaque Ansari rose to great heights in politics. During the period of the first Chief Minister of Bihar, Dr. Sri Krishna Sinha, he was elected M.L.C. from local bodies' constituency in the year 1958. After more than two decades, he was nominated to the Bihar Legislative Council in 1984 by Chief Minister, Chandra Sekhar Singh. In the year 1991, Chief Minister, Dr. Jagannath Mishra included A. Razzaque Ansari in his cabinet.

The story of Abdur Razzaque Ansari's life is that of struggle and dedication. Imagine the case of a simple handloom weaver working hard in the handloom pit for late hours and through out day, if needed. Producing handloom fabrics to earn his livelihood was not the only concern but marketing of that produce was of more uphill task in those days. Being an extremely backward area with no mode of communication, Razzaque Ansari had to put his load of handloom fabrics on his back and used to go to Ranchi, travelling a stretch of 13 kilometers of unbuilt and uneven road on foot to sell his products. It was the dignity of labour, he believed, which rewarded him a life of respect and dignity in later years of his life.

Himself being the Chairman, supported by the active presence of a group of selfless and dedicated band of secretaries of the cooperative Handloom Societies affiliated, the Chotanagpur Regional Handloom Cooperative Union flourished. It had a very impressive sprawling area to house the Union together with other related facilities needed. It always remained humming with activities.

For all the leaders of the Momin movement in Bihar who happened to be my senior colleagues, I had the best of personal relations with Abdur Razzaque Ansari that stretched a span of more than forty years. We had very clear understanding about each other, both very close to A.Q. Ansari. We never allowed misunderstanding to come in the way of our relationship. Though senior in age, he was always so nice to me that he gave me respect and regard which I owed with a great sense of humility. It was entirely because of this basic fact that after his death in the year

1992, I wholeheartedly supported his second son, Manzoor Ahmad Ansari, whom he had groomed in his life time to succeed him in politics, Momin and handloom movements.

I would like to share with the readers the happenings of the last day of his life which was in a sense dedicated to the cause of Momin Conference. After the death of Z.R. Ansari, Abdur Rauf Ansari, a veteran Congressman and Momin Conference leader from West Bengal was elected president of All India Momin Conference. On the fateful day, Razzaque Ansari came over to Patna and stayed in his flat in Udaigiri opposite Patna Museum. He invited me and Abdur Rauf Ansari from Calcutta to pour his heart before us. He suffered from heart ailment and had already several strokes. He said that his health now does not permit him to continue with active participation in Momin movement.

He, therefore, suggested that henceforth his second son Manzoor Ahmad Ansari who till now was in central government services, will be with you. He further said that he has purchased one Bolero for use for State Momin Conference which will facilitate the movement. His words made us depressed but we simply accepted his proposal with nods. The same evening, March 14, 1992, he alongwith Abdur Rauf Ansari, left for Ranchi and Calcutta respectively by the same flight. In the late hours of that very night, I got the most shocking news of his death at Ranchi after a massive heart attack.

Razzaque Ansari was given state funeral at his village, Irba. Dr. Jagannath Mishra, leader of opposition and former chief minister, attended his funeral.

Abdur Razzaque Ansari was a religious person. He was soft spoken and admired by one and all. He left behind a happy family of sons and daughters under the care of their mother, a pious lady. His eldest son Sayeed Ahmad Ansari was an officer with a private bank posted at Calcutta. His second son, Manzoor Ahmad Ansari had by now matured as a handloom movement activist. The Regional Handloom Weaver's Cooperative Union had a turn over of Rs. 5 crores. His sons unanimously decided to set up a most modern hospital at Irba as a memorial to their father, Abdur Razzaque Ansari. Like his father, Sayeed Ahmad Ansari is an enterprising person. As a first step, he first resigned from bank service and came back to Ranchi. They decided to construct a super hospital of the level of Apollo Hospital. It was certainly an uphill task. Another important decision they took was that it will be named after their father as 'Abdur Razzaque Ansari Memorial Weaver's Hospital' to be built as a subsidiary of the Chotanagpur Regional Handloom Cooperative Union. They laboured hard to obtain loans from Banks and other agencies, including Ministry of Textiles, Government of India. I had also my share of efforts in this direction. Both, I and Manzoor had very close and cordial relations with Union Textile Minister, G. Venkataswamy, a veteran Congress leader and a very noble soul from Andhra Pradesh. We always enjoyed his blessings and support in the party affairs. He wanted to help the proposed hospital at Irba. The then Textile Secretary was later elevated as the Union Cabinet Secretary. There was a fund lying in the Textile Ministry for the welfare of weavers. Venkataswamy asked us to come to his ministry, which we did. He called Textile Secretary and asked us to explain everything. I made a strong plea with the Textile Secretary before the minister to provide substantial financial assistance to the Chotanagpur Regional Handloom Coop. Union to help raise a super hospital for the medical welfare of the weavers of the region. My plea was so strong in its substance and appeal that the secretary was fully convinced and told the minister that the fund available with the minister can be allotted for the purpose.

Besides G. Venkataswamy's support, we had the blessings of the Governor Dr. A.R. Kidwai to our great advantage. Dr. Kidwai was always ready to go to any length to help the weavers of the state and the Momin community, at large, being the nationalist group. He had great admiration for the role played by the Momin community in the freedom movement.

Coming back, Abdul Qaiyum Ansari had yet another person in Hafiz Manzoor Hussain whom he respected the most. Hafiz Manzoor Hussain, a deeply religious man from Kochus, near Sasaram was the son of Shamshul Ulema Maulana Mohammad Yahya, one of the founders of Momin Conference. Hafiz Manzoor Hussain became MLA in the first assembly elections.

Other Muslim organizations including Imarat Sharia, Jamiatul Ulema, and Maulana Sajjad's Muslim Independent Party (MIP) were against Muslim League. During 1937 elections, the Muslim Independent party led by Maulana Mohammad Sajjad won largest number of reserved Muslim seats, but after his death in 1940, MIP faded away. On the eve of 1946 election on separate electorate when Rajendra Prasad worried over the fate of the 40 Muslim seats, noted that of the Congress Muslims, the MIP, the Jamiat Ulema-e-Hind and Momin Conference, the only active body was Momin Conference. Papiya Ghosh wrote in her book, 'Community & Nation'. "The Muslim League had been able to dupe the other Muslim organizations but not the Momin Conference." — "The Momin Conference projected itself as an organization that had redeemed the Biradri from the backwaters and made it conscious of its power without clashing with the British."

Papiya Ghosh quoting a page from the history, writes — "After Sajjad's death in 1940, though MIP faded out from electoral stage that it occupied in 1937, it was a member of the Bihar Muslim Parliamentary Board formed at a meeting in Khanqauh Rahmani in Monghyr, alongwith Muslim League, Momin Conference and Jamiatul Ulema, Bihar."

The decision of Momin leadership to do away with its political character after independence coupled with clarion call by the leadership to the Momin community to join Congress party strengthened the party as well as the position of the Momin leaders in the Congress party. Groups other than the Momin Conference which supported Congress party during the assembly elections on the basis of separate electorate could not enjoy the same political privilege. However, in Bihar, the Muslim League stalwart Syed Jafar Imam was taken into the Bihar cabinet after a general decision of the Congress High Command to provide amnesty to Muslim League leaders left in India.

Besides the Muslims in the Congress party, Congress could not afford to ignore Muslims belonging to the Momin community because of their unparallel contribution. The political battle during pre-independence days was mainly fought in the state of U.P., Bihar and Bengal where Muslim League had stronghold. The Momin Conference gave a very strong fight against the Muslim League and its agenda of the division of the country. Every section of Congress leadership had high appreciation for the support of the Momin Conference and the Momin community for the Congress party and fully reciprocated during distribution of party tickets for assembly or Lok Sabha elections or in cases of nomination to the upper houses in states and at the centre or even during cabinet formation and gave due representation to Momin community. While Abdul Qaiyum Ansari and Abul Ahad Mohammad Noor were in the Bihar cabinet, Abdur Rauf Ansari in Bengal cabinet and Istefa Hussain Ansari of Gorakhpur was in U.P. ministry. Md. Ibrahim Ansari was the cabinet minister of Andhra Pradesh. Apart from that, in U.P., Bihar and West Bengal, there were a number of Momin MLAs in state legislatures and upper houses. Yusuf Ansari won Lok Sabha election from Siwan parliamentary seat and was returned five consecutive times. He was the most popular leader of the constituency and none of the other candidates could stand successful against him. In later years, Maulvi Saminuddin from Banka, Maulvi Shafiqullah Ansari and later, Maulvi Abdul Hannan Ansari from Madhubani became Members of Parliament. When Chandra Sekhar Singh was the chief minister, who had high regards for the role of the Momin community in the national freedom movement, literally picked up Salahuddin Ansari, a lecturer and son of Yasin Ansari, M.L.A of Santhal Pargana, gave him ticket during parliamentary elections from Godda and vigorously campaigned to see him elected.

A very significant point to note is that in early years after independence, those among the Momin community whom Congress party provided tickets for Bihar assembly were mostly religious persons. They were the people in the forefront of the Momin movement. For example, Maulana Sami Nadvi was first elected M.L.A. and later nominated M.L.C. who became cabinet minister in Bihar, had done his Madarsa education from Nadva, and Hafiz Idris Ansari, M.L.A. from Dhaka, East Champaran was made minister of state by Kedar Pandey. Maulvi Saminuddin was Member of Parliament from Banka. Abdul Qaiyum Ansari, an extremely religious person was the paternal grandson of Maulana Abdullah Ghazipuri, a distinguished Islamic scholar who had authored book on Wahabi Fiqah. In the state of Uttar Pradesh, Maulvi Habibur Rahman Nomani, M.L.C, was the son of renowned Islamic scholar, Maulana Abdul Latif.

Handloom Industry: The presence of Ansari and Noor in Bihar cabinet facilitated flourishing of the handloom industry in Bihar. The handloom centres at Biharsharif, Sigouri, Madhubani, Manpur, Jamal Hata in Siwan, Sitamarhi, Bhagalpur, Ranchi and other places, were throbbing with life. Handloom cooperative societies were formed throughout the state and were affiliated to one apex organization at Patna. Weavers in the fold of cooperatives got freedom from middle men who so far exploited the weavers. The weaver's Cooperative societies had the privilege to get yarn from the apex body at reasonable prices from yarn centres spread over the entire state, thus freeing weavers from the clutches of 'Mahajans'. The products of the weavers co-operative societies were purchased by the apex handloom organization which were sold through their network of emporia throughout the state. Through this co-operative mechanism, the weavers in the cooperative fold had no tension about the 'Mahajans', and used to get yarn at reasonable prices and had nothing to worry about marketing of their finished goods. It was the golden period for handloom industry in the country. When the fist non-congress government took over in Bihar, the effectiveness of the State cooperative body of Handlooms was weakened by making half a dozen cooperative unions in the state out of political consideration. It was more a political decision. Most of these bodies, instead of catering the needs of the weavers of their respective regions, merely became centres of corruption.

It was the basic policy of the Union government (Congress) to revive the traditional handloom and khadi industries of the country. The handloom fabrics are always in great demand in European countries and India became the largest exporter of handlooms. Handloom fabrics are always the earner of foreign exchange for the country.

Two factors became responsible for the deterioration of the handloom-powerloom industry in the country. After 1967, the non-congress coalition governments in the states had biased attitude towards Congress and the handloom industry. While in the South, the handloom industry stood on strong turf so it survived this attitude of the government. Moreover, in the South, overwhelming weavers were from the Hindu community but in Hindi states, Muslim weavers were mostly engaged in the industry. So, they had to face the political brunt of the non-congress parties in power. The weavers as a community were known traditionally as nationalists and pro-Congress. While deciding the policy of the governments, this factor went against the weavers and the handloom industry. However, inspite of this difference between South and North, handloom industry in the entire country faced general apathy of the government.

The handloom industry in Bihar and for that matter, the Momin community of the state had a bitter taste of political bias after the fall of Congress government and coming to power of Lalu Prasad who remained in the saddle of power for fifteen years. It was the darkest period of handloom industry in Bihar since independence. Some Muslim leaders of his party convinced him that since Momin leaders will never support him politically; it was of no political advantage to give any government attention towards development of handlooms. As a result, the handloom industry of the state starved of financial assistance. Vibrant handloom centres at Sigouri, Biharsharif, Madhubani, Bhagalpur, Siwan etc. started showing signs of deterioration. There was a significant fall of handloom production. Weavers were compelled to switch on to other sources of earning bread and a considerable number of them migrated to neighbouring state of U.P.

Apart from this political discrimination, the greatest problem faced by the weavers was that of frequent hike in yarn prices. It always remained a phenomenon at national level. The All India Handloom Board was seized with this problem. The government took a concrete step towards this direction and opened a National Handloom Development Corporation with its headquarters at Lucknow which continues to be vibrant. When Khurshid Alam Khan was the Union Textile Minister, he took deep personal interest to solve the problem of hike in yarn prices. On his personal initiative, the All India Handloom Board constituted a Yarn Sub-Committee out of its members to formulate ways and means for overcoming this chronic problem faced by the weavers. The author was one of its members. The Sub-Committee toured different parts of the country, interacted with the weavers, officials and NGOs. After lot of discussions and burning the midnight oil, the sub-committee brought out very comprehensive and workable formulae in the direction to solve the problem in an effective manner. The report might be lying in the achieves of the union ministry of textiles. The scheme presented to the government through the All India Handloom Board however, never implemented; reasons always remained beyond my knowledge. A great frustration for me, indeed. The problem still continues to be there.

There is a long history of exploitation of the weavers by the middle men and that continues with all its ferocity. The government has been spending a lot on the development of handlooms but not in an organized manner and needed planning, however, there are masters in the art of scams and scandals who leave no opportunity to swindle crores of government money meant for the development of handlooms and handloom weavers. In fact, the huge financial assistance through different schemes was not reaching to the weavers. As a result, the weavers continue to having hard days in U.P. and Bihar.

Somappa from South was a legendry figure of handloom cooperatives in the country. He established an apex handloom cooperative body at the national level and set up Handloom Houses in metropolitan cities. The national handloom cooperative body under Somappa flourished out of his dedicated efforts. The Handloom Houses, which marketed the best products of handlooms collected from different parts of the country, were hot favourites for handloom lovers. Somappa had a good number of most influential persons from states on the board of his apex organization. During his period, this apex organization was considered prestigious. Abdul Qaiyum Ansari was one of the members of this pioneer cooperative body. After Somappa died, things started to deteriorate. Some unscrupulous persons managed to make entrance into the body and hijacked this prestigious organization for self goodwill. It became a sick organization. I remember when Margaret Thatcher was the Prime Minister of UK, she complained to Indira Gandhi while she was on a tour of that country, about the fraud in the export of handloom fabrics from India to UK as non-handloom cloth mostly powerloom cloth was exported.

The Congress government at the centre in early years after independence set up yarn mills in the states to facilitate supply of yarn to the handloom weavers. While these mills did a good job of catering yarn to the weavers at reasonable prices, later most of the mills either became victims of mismanagement or corrupt practices. In U.P., the Chairman of the Etawah Spinning Mill, who happened to be incidentally from the Momin community, earned a bad name. He was accused of corrupt practices and so was removed from the chairmanship.

In Bihar, due to the efforts of Abdul Qaiyum Ansari and Abul Ahad Mohammad Noor, spinning mill in cooperative sector was established at Mokamah, 60 kms away from the state capital, which remained vibrant for a long period and served the handloom weavers of the state. After their death, the spinning mill became non-functional.

For almost three decades after India won freedom, the Momin community in India was the most favoured community for the ruling Congress party. And there were genuine reasons for that. The Momin Conference, as a separate political entity, stood firmly against the communal politics of Muslim league and its demand for homeland for Indian Muslims. Momin Conference was alone in the field and none of the other small Muslim groups, not even Jamiat Ulema, could give electoral fight to Muslim League during separate electorate. This honour went to Momin Conference alone. Momin Conference and for that, the Momin community risked everything worth its name to uphold the ideals of secularism and Hindu-Muslim unity. There was tremendous appreciation in the country for the Momin community who had fought out communal tendencies of the Muslim League. It was the Momin Conference that trashed the Muslim League's allegation that Congress was a party of Hindus. And because of this ground reality, the pro-Muslim League and non-Congress Muslims became inimical to Momin community. They even branded Ansaris as 'Kafirs' for their support to 'Hindu Congress' and according to their outlook, jeopardizing political interest of Indian Muslims. They could not reconcile themselves with the changed political situation of the country where Muslims had to learn to live in harmony with the Hindu majority. This section of the Muslim community was jealous of Congress Muslims in general and Momin Conference and its leaders, A.Q. Ansari and A.A.M. Noor, in particular.

The apathy of the Congress towards Urdu and other serious issues related to the Muslim community were causing anxiety to Momin leadership. Ansari was bold enough to set up Congress Muslim Front in the state to highlight the grievances of the aggrieved community with himself as its chairman. Veteran Congress leaders A.A.M. Noor, Maulana Shah Noorullah, M.L.C.; Manzoor Ahmad Ejazi, MLA; Captain Shah Jehan, M.L.A. from Gaya; Maulana Mohiuddin Nadvi, Editor, *Sadaqaut* (Urdu) Daily; Syed Anisur Rahman, Dumri Kothi, and others were prominent members of the front. I and Shamael Nabi were Secretaries of the front. Amongst active members were comrade Habibur Rahman and Haroon Rashid who formed the close coterie around Ansari. There was murmuring in the Congress circles over the action of Ansari for setting up a separate front within the Congress but the Congress High Command dared not to question Ansari on the issue. These veteran nationalist leaders were determined to fight the case of the Muslim community of the state from this separate platform.

Apart from that, Ansari and Noor, decided to highlight the problems of the Muslim community of the state through the platform of the Momin Conference as well. They agreed to hold a one-day conference at Anjuman Islamia Hall on August 9, 1965. Delegates from different parts of the state, those of the Momin community descended at Patna to attend the conference. Quite unaware of behind the scene conspiracy cooking up in nearby Muslim dominant Subzibagh area, which was then the hot bed of Muslim politics, participants were pouring in the Anjuman Islamia Hall. K.B. Sahay was then the chief minister of the state who inaugurated the conference. A group of young Muslims belonging to the so-called upper caste, were shouting against Ansari and other organisers at the main entrance to the conference venue. They were agitating against the remark of the Momin leaders who had allegedly labelled 90 per cent upper caste Muslims as communal. A senior Urdu journalist though from the backward Muslim community but a bitter opponent of A.Q. Ansari was the moving spirit behind this violent agitation. Since, it was the main thoroughfare and the centre of political activities of Patna, the crowd swelled up. The whole atmosphere became tense as the crowd started hurling abuses and booed and jeered those coming to the venue. Some prominent Momin leaders including Maulvi Saminuddin. Latifur Rahman from Nagmatia, Maulana Sami Nadvi, Rezaur Rahman Ansari, Advocate became victims of the violent fury of the protestors. Maulvi Saminuddin who was later elected to Lok Sabha and Sardar Latifur Rahman, who was well known for his affiliation with Muslim League, were manhandled and the rowdy crowd spit on their beards. The senior S.P., incidentally a Muslim, who was present at the venue to maintain law and order where the chief minister and a number of ministers and a host of VIPs were present, completely failed in his duty. There was total inaction of the police and the hoodlums were allowed to carry on with their violent mission. When the news about violence and beating of delegates reached inside Anjuman Islamia Hall, there was anger and the audience wanted to chase away the violent protestors. Ansari shouted on the agitated members to hold back and not to react but to keep patience and peace. Ansari knew that it was their game plan to tarnish his image and bring a bad name to the organisation; therefore, he never wanted that delegates in any way react.

The conference was abruptly ended to meet the next day at 9 in the morning. The administration heaved a sigh of relief as Ansari's initiative had averted backlash that might have resulted in large scale bloodshed. But for his strong warning to his people otherwise the situation of Patna would have been altogether different. Ansari continued to be in Rajendra surgical ward of Patna Medical College Hospital for treatment of his fractured arm, a place just behind the venue of occurrence, Anjuman Islamia Hall. That evening, as usual, he came out on the lawns of the hospital by the side of flowing Ganges. A stream of leaders made a bee line to express solidarity with A.Q. Ansari. The Chief Minister with I.G. Police arrived. Next was J.N. Sahu, Patna D.M. and the Senior S.P. Fazal Ahmad, whose son's name was being talked about for leading the violent mob. The Chief Minister was apologetic for the inaction of the police and so, also the I.G. Police. They, however, thanked Ansari for the maintenance of peaceful atmosphere out of his initiative. At this point, Ansari's anger burst and he could not hold himself. Pointing his finger to Senior S.P., Ansari said that this young beautiful person in uniform is a worthless police officer who should be thrown into the Ganges. Everybody was silent and Fazal Ahmad stood motionless. Sensing the awkwardness of the situation, I.G. Police whispered him to leave. Patna Collector J.N. Sahu assured Ansari that the rioters were being identified and no body was going to be spared.

Morning newspapers prominently carried the news giving dozens of names arrested for their violent role and lodged in Bankipore jail that included prominent anti-Congress elements including son of a cabinet minister who was erstwhile Muslim League leader, another son of a vice-chancellor and more significantly son of the senior S.P. of Patna. The large scale arrests made sent shock waves to the citizens of the state capital. It is said that someone who had enmity, political or otherwise, took this opportunity to give some names to the police though they were innocent and get them arrested out of revenge. However, after these arrests, there was hush hush silence every where in the state capital.

The session on the next day opened with the speech of Ansari who thanked the audience for maintaining peace. Ansari made a memorable speech as he thundered that the unfortunate happenings at the state conference of nationalist Muslims held in the historic Anjuman Islamia Hall in which dozens of senior delegates got cuts and bruises was pointer to the ground reality that even two decades after the country got divided, there still exist 'Pakistani nests' here and there. He declared that he has been fighting against such bigoted elements before independence and shall continue to fight with the same zeal. Ansari said that he was not going to be browbeaten by such elements. Those who got the pinch of it, Ansari's speech left them fuming.

Undeterred with the happenings, the leaders of the Congress Muslim Front decided to meet Prime Minister of India, Lal Bahadur Shastri to discuss with him the burning issues of the Muslims of the state and present him a memorandum. Consequently, a jumbo size delegation of nationalist Muslims left for Delhi with Ansari as its leader. Prominent among those in the delegation were Manzoor Ahsan Ejazi, Captain Shah Jahan, Maulana Syed Noorullah, Maulana Mohiuddin Nadvi. A.A.M. Noor, Haroon Rashid, Shamael Nabi, Comrade Habibur Rahman and the author.

A very significal point of the Momin movement during the period of A.Q. Ansari was that the network spread over in majority of the states. He ruled over the hearts of the Momin-Ansar community of the country. Ansari was the most respected. He reached out to his people and extensively toured besides Bihar, different areas in U.P. including Lucknow, Allahabad, Varanasi, Bhadohi, Bombay, and Jabalpur. The author accompanied him almost on all organizational tours. We went to Bombay number of times. Despite all facilities to stay at Ciruit House being a minister, he always preferred to stay with his friend and General Secretary of AIMC, Sayeed. A. Shaikh. It was once during such visits to Bombay that the author along Ansari Saheb and Sayeed Shaikh met the Editor of Inquilab (Urdu) daily and legendry Momin figure of older times, Abdul Hameed Ansari. At Bhadohi, the carpet centre, though we stayed with the carpet baron of those days and his namesake, Abdul Qaiyum Ansari he took the opportunity to meet his relatives. For me, the one advantage of the tours with Ansari Saheb was that I got introduced to the leaders and activists of the Momin Conference everywhere. People identified me with Momin movement.

Jawahar Lal Nehru was an admirer of Momin movement.

Within party forum, Nehru, on such occasions as warranted, was always found paying tributes to the Momin community, the most depressed class of the Muslims for their role in the freedom movement, which he described as 'unprecedented' and 'unbelievable'. He personally knew A.Q. Ansari and had on occasions the opportunity to interact with him. Indira Gandhi politically groomed under her father, knew all about Momin movement and A.Q. Ansari. But she never demonstrated her honesty in dealing with Ansari community or its leader, A.Q. Ansari as the Chairperson of the party or the Prime Minister of India.

Once it so happened that a senior most journalist, Shambhu Nath Jha, news editor of English daily of Patna, *The Searchlight* (now seized its publication) came down to meet Ansari at his Chajju Bagh residence in Patna holding a copy of Delhi edition of 'Statesman.' It carried a front page story about the probable names under consideration for the post of the vice-president of India. Only two names were mentioned, one was that of Justice Hidayatullah and another name was that of A.Q. Ansari of Bihar. Ansari had a smile on his face but did not show any sign of joyous reaction. However, Shambhu Babu was quite optimistic and wanted that Ansari should not loose time and air dash to Delhi to meet Congress high command and lobby for himself. Ansari took his advice in a casual manner. Ansari told Shambhu Babu that if he was a Congress high command choice, nothing will come in the way and plainly said that he never believed in political lobbying.

In Bihar politics, over the years, Ansari grew as the most accepted leader of all the factions of the state Congress. Lalit Narayan Mishra was a great admirer of Ansari and respected him most. Mishra was a dynamic leader and was able to create for himself a place of importance in the coterie around Indira Gandhi. He was considered the most influential leader of Bihar at the centre. Mishra wanted Ansari to be drafted in the government at the central level. For sometime, he was lobbying for Ansari with Prime Minister. During his visits to Patna, Mishra used to confer with Ansari. Once when Ansari was not in any of the state houses, Mishra pleaded with Ansari to shift to Delhi for nomination to a vacant seat in Rajya Sabha. Ansari was reluctant and did not want to leave Bihar politics but Mishra overconfident, insisted that Indiraji had agreed to induct him in the union cabinet. Ansari reluctantly agreed. Ansari was nominated to Rajya Sabha but never made a union minister. After the term expired, Ansari came back to Bihar politics. Lalit Nayan Mishra was himself unhappy as he could not do anything concrete for Ansari Saheb. But he was never frustrated. He continued his efforts to place Ansari at the top.

State assembly elections were held and Ansari was once again returned from his home constituency Dehri-on-Sone. As usual, hectic parleys for leader of Congress legislature party were in process. Mishra told Ansari that Indira Gandhi had agreed to his proposal to favour you as the leader of the state legislature party. Since, he could not be accommodated in the central ministry, she now wanted him to be leader of the party. Mishra was quite confident of his proposal. As the date of election came nearer, we noticed Mishra again making frequent trips between Patna and Delhi. On the other hand, Ansari was calm and never demonstrated his curiosity for the post nor did he lobby for himself with congress legislators. In fact, he showed quite indifference to all such activities. The D day had come. Every one in the party knew that Ansari was the choice and was poised to be next chief minister of the state. Gulzari Lal Nanda, Union Minister was the observer. After formal speech expressing the necessity of maintenance of unity in the party, Nanda dramatically took out a piece of paper from his pocket suggesting that Indiraji had given this name for election as the party leader. Everybody held his or her breath. Next moment, he announced the name of Kedar Pandey. All present were taken by surprise and shocked. Ansari was the senior most in the party and had unblemished record of service. He was a man of integrity and commanded great respect. If nominated, he would have been a unanimous choice of the legislators. Though ditched by the High Command, Ansari never showed his annoyance and kept cool. Newly elected leader Kedar Pandey realized the level of humiliation for Ansari when it was almost certain that there will merely be formal announcement of Ansari as his name was around in the party circles for the last few weeks. Moreover, Lalit Narарayan Mishra had spared no efforts to see Ansari as the chief minister of the state. He was overconfident that this time his mission will not fail. Kedar Pandey was too junior to Ansari Saheb and the fact is that when Ansari joined cabinet for the first time in 1946, Kedar Pandey was a student. However, Kedar Pandey now wanted to include Ansari in his cabinet. He requested Ansari but he politely, and firmly, refused. People of his Dehri constituency close to Ansari were furious at the injustice of the Congress High Command. They strongly opposed Kedar Pandey's efforts to induct Ansari in his cabinet. Kedar Pandey was a clever person. He continued his efforts and tried utmost to persuade Ansari. Ansari was a gentle soul. He could not resist for long and ultimately gave way. He was made an irrigation minister.

After Lalit Narayan Mishra succumbed to bomb attack in Samastipur, Congress High Command directed Kedar Pandey to include his younger brother, Dr. Jagannath Mishra in the state cabinet. Kedar Pandey did a political somersault, took away irrigation department from Ansari and allotted it to the most junior minister, Dr. Jagannath Mishra. It was most shocking as Ansari was humiliated at the hands of a junior minister.

It was the Muslim festival of Id-ul-Azha commonly known as Bakrid. Ansari got news that Amyar *Bundh* in his constituency had burst, flooding agricultural land. He immediately decided to visit the place next day and come back by evening. As he got down from his car and walked a few steps, he was hit by massive heart attack. Within no time, he collapsed and expired. The news of his death spread like a wildfire. A sheet of gloom covered the entire state.

The family decided his burial in Dehri-on-Sone. His body was first brought to Patna and kept in the verandah of his official residence at 1, Chajju Bagh. Ministers, officials, even judges and people from all walks of life passed by his body to pay respect to such a noble soul. Ansari Saheb's Namaz-e-Janaza was held at Anjuman Islamia Hall. His body was later taken in a police truck followed by cars to Dehri-on-Sone. He was given state funeral. Tens of thousands of people from Patna and his constituency thronged the place of his burial.

He was such a popular figure amongst the masses that his death shocked everybody. Everywhere in the Congress circle, it was on everybody's lips that Ansari could not bear a number of successive shocks of utter injustice to his dismay. He was the tallest of tall political persons of the country. First, his name went round as a probable choice of Congress High command for vice-president of India, next he could not find his way in the union cabinet as was most expected and finally, his election as the leader of the Congress legislature party was frustrated at the last moment. And to crown all that, his greatest friend, admirer and supporter in the party, L.N. Mishra was murdered.

With the demise of Abdul Qaiyum Ansari, the golden era of the Momin movement ended abruptly. Momin community all over was stunned over this heavy loss. He served the community and the state with dedication. He had an unblemished record of service to the people of all shades of life. The state Congress and Congress Muslims had suffered a heavy loss. He was a noble soul who was always ready to help persons facing problems. Every one, even the persons of the level of Muslim officers, who were victims of discrimination, found solace in Ansari as he was always ready to help for the right cause. However, it was the Momin community which was at its greatest loss since it was left directionless. A.A.M. Noor had lost his closest colleague of the Momin movement. For everybody, it was frustration as to who will lead such a big community and the movement.

Election of Z.R. Ansari

Hafiz Manzoor Hussain who was then the general secretary of the Momin Conference at the national level, called an urgent meeting of the Conference at Patna to elect new president.

With the announcement of date and venue for the election of new president, being a viable organization, lobbying for candidates started in full swing. There was no probable candidate in Bihar and Bengal and we all looked towards Uttar Pradesh. There were three persons in that state. The senior most was Istefa Hussain Ansari of Gorakhpur. He later became cabinet minister in the state. He was a distant relation of Hafiz Manzoor Hussain. His son Akhtar Hussain Ansari, who retired as an officer of the Bihar government was married in Allahabad, related to Istefa Hussain Saheb. Maulvi Habibur Rahman Nomani was also an old activist of Momin movement in U.P. from Mau. He was the chairman of Itawah Spinning Mill. Maulvi Nomani later became M.L.C. in U.P. He was the most serious contender but unfortunately, he was a controversial figure and there was none in the working committee to support his candidature. The third person was Ziaur Rahman Ansari from Unnao. Like Istefa Hussain, Z.R. Ansari also came from a nationalist Muslim family. His father Habibur Rahman contested his first election as a Congress candidate against Muslim League in 1946 and trounced him to become a member of lower house of state legislature in U.P. In 1952 general elections, he was again elected to the U.P. assembly and became MLA for the second time.

Younger of the three candidates, Z.R. Ansari had recently won Lok Sabha seat and inducted as Dy. Minister, Petroleum in the union cabinet. He was first elected to the U.P. assembly in 1962 and became member of Lok Sabha from Unnao. He came from a family of nationalists but the only drawback was that he was not fully involved in the activities of the Momin Conference as such. Istefa Hussain and Nomani were known figures and Momin leaders knew them but Z.R. Ansari was not known to most of the members of the working committee or other Momin leaders. However, I had known him personally since long. During our visits to Lucknow a number of times, I and A.Q. Ansari used to visit Darul Shafa, U.P. M.L.A. hostel where Nasim Ansari and Z.R. Ansari were mostly found in flat 27/B.

In Patna, meeting of the working committee was scheduled in the headquarters of the Bihar State Handloom Weaver's Co-operative Union at Exhibition Road. The younger group of lobbyists included Khalid Rashid Saba, me and Abdul Qaiyum Ansari of Bhagalpur. There was an under current feeling that Hafiz Manzoor Hussain, the national General Secretary wanted Istefa Hussain of Gorakhpur, Uttar Pradesh being a senior man, to succeed Ansari Saheb. On our part, we wanted that since Z.R. Ansari was in the Lok Sabha and was in the government as Dy. Minister, he can be of immense help to the community at this juncture when we had lost a person of the stature of Ansari Saheb. We were confident that our contention was strong, justified and will be appealing to the members. In fact, there was not so apparent lobbying for Istefa Hussain and if any, were just behind the scene. However, there were no takers for the candidature of Maulvi Habibur Rahman Nomani, a veteran Momin leader from Mau, Uttar Pradesh. He stood nowhere. We started our campaign with the giant political figure Abul Ahad Mohammad Noor. We gathered courage to open our mouth before him, a difficult job indeed. Surprisingly, he listened to us patiently without rebutting us as his temperament was. He advised us to speak to other members when they arrive for the meeting. We were happy that he did not show his usual anger and was so polite. We could make out that he was also in favour of Z.R. Ansari's candidature. We did not stop there and, I rang up Istefa Hussain and enquired about his detailed programme of arrival at Patna. He was scheduled to reach Patna a day before the meeting from Gorakhpur by train and across the Ganges, through steamer to Digha Ghat in Patna. Likewise, I rang up Z.R. Ansari also to know his mind and also programme of coming to Patna. He was a serious contender.

I made it possible to be present at Digha Ghat to receive Istefa Hussain. No other person was there to receive him not even the host where he had to stay. He was happy that someone else other than the host was there. He told me that he was to stay with Akhtar Ahmad Ansari. I accompanied him on his rickshaw for a distance. He asked me about the election situation and during the talk, emphatically denied that he was also a candidate. I told him that it was surprising as Hafiz Manzoor Hussain and his men were campaigning for him which could not have been without his consent. He once again denied that he was interested in the elections. He went further ahead and said that a young person like Ziaur Rahman Ansari should be made next president. The things were quite clear now and I felt very much relieved. Back to my group when I gave this news there was a sense of jubilation that now our candidate was sure to win.

A day before election, veteran Momin leader and one of its founders Abu Shams Abdul Ghafoor with others had arrived from Calcutta and stayed with Abul Ahad Mohammad Noor. We met him and his team and strongly pleaded the case of Z.R. Ansari. Haji Saheb smiled and asked us to keep utmost peace at the venue of election and should see that election is carried out in a most dignified atmosphere.

In the morning of the election day, Z.R. Ansari reached Patna by flight. I was there to receive him. I noticed Maulvi Nomani was also alighting from the Delhi flight.

I briefed Ziaur Rahman about the election situation especially in reference to Istefa Hussain's clear denial about his candidature. I told him that Nomani is no where in the picture as not a single member is in his favour; therefore decks were cleared for his unanimous election. He was glad to know these developments as he was apprehending that Istefa Hussain will give him tough fight. The Working Committee meeting was held in a solemn and peaceful atmosphere. Glowing tributes were paid to Abdul Qaiyum Ansari who, during his tenure which was full of tribulations, steered away the movement to great heights. A resolution to this effect was passed.

Mr. Z.R. Ansari was the only choice of the members as such he was elected uncontested. Like previous occasions in the history of Momin Conference, the election of the president was smooth and in peaceful environment. Momin Conference maintained its high traditions.

Z.R. Ansari Era

With the sudden demise of Abdul Qaiyum Ansari and election of Z.R. Ansari, another era of the post independence Momin movement began. The leadership now travelled to the neighbouring state of Uttar Pradesh and all eyes were focussed on the new incumbent Ziaur Rahman Ansari. Though the new president hailed from U.P., but since he was a central minister, Delhi was now his permanent place of stay.

As is natural, there was a sudden spurt in the activities of the Momin movement activists and leaders of Uttar Pradesh. They made a bee line to Delhi to meet the new president to find a place in the new scheme of things. Prominent Momin leaders of the state including Maulana Habibur Rahman Nomani, Istefa Hussain Ansari, Abid Ali, Md. Nesar from Tanda, Md. Nasim Ansari, Md. Amin Ansari, Mau-Aema, Ashfaque Vaziri and a host of others wanted ZR to give them due place in the central and provincial working committees.

By then, a new Momin leadership from Andhra Pradesh had appeared from behind the scene. It was Kasim Ali Abid who was recently nominated as a Rajya Sabha member of the Congress party. It was entirely a new name for the Momin leaders. Both Abdul Qaiyum Ansari, when he himself was a Rajya Sabha member and Z.R. Ansari were instrumental in Qasim Ali Abid's nomination to the upper house. Being a candidate from the Momin community, he expected support from the two top most Momin leaders. He had struck the right cord. Both A.Q. Ansari and Z.R. Ansari had full support of his candidature before the Congress High command. Being now a Rajya Sabha member, he expected top place in the central working committee of the Momin Conference.

Z.R. Ansari was siezed with the immediate task to reshape the Working Committee of the AIMC (All India Momin Conference) as he was constantly under pressure. But the problem with the new president was that he had little knowledge about the national leaders baring those from Uttar Pradesh. He had great hopes in me since he knew that I was in the movement for a long time moreover I was so closely associated with the departed leader. Z.R. Ansari had bigger plans to put Momin movement to great heights. He was amazed to know that till now there was no office of the AIMC. But he had no realization about the fact that Abdul Qaiyum Ansari was a towering political personality besides a very popular Momin leader commanding great respect and regard in the community. He was most successful Momin leader since the time of its inception. A.Q. Ansari never found any difficulty in the absence of a full fledged office. But now with the changed situation, it was a must.

The new president wanted to discuss organizational issues with me to have the latest position of the movement. A lot of matters related to Momin Conference were discussed during my two day stay there. ZR showed his anxiety to go fast and wanted to hold national session of the AIMC as for more than two decades after Patna session it could not be held. He had many plans in his mind, some feasible and others not.

During the discussions, he wanted me to shift over to Delhi temporarily to give him a helping hand to make Momin conference a viable organization. I was hesitant to accept his proposal as my family was at Patna. I was actively associated with newspaper. I was the Editor of '*Sada-e-Hind*'. Moreover, my mother was sick and needed my presence at Patna. I came back to Patna but ZR was still hopeful. He continued to put moral pressure on me. He assured providing all facilities including a vehicle at my disposal, accommodation, etc. I was in a dilemma what to do. Going to Delhi means discontinuing my paper, I was at a fix. It amounted to a big sacrifice on my part for the cause of the Momin movement. Ultimately, ZR succeeded and he literally lifted me to Delhi. I had to stop publication of my paper, '*Sada-e-Hind*' at Patna, a great loss to me and my reputation as a journalist. My younger brother was in Delhi serving Delhi administration as an I.A.S. officer. He had his own official accommodation in civil lines area and wanted me to stay with him. However, it could not be possible. ZR personally requested Prime Minister Indira Gandhi to provide accommodation for the central office of the AIMC at Delhi as he wanted to organize the Momin Conference with new zeal. Indira

Gandhi needed the support of Momin community in her difficult political situation as during freedom movement. She ordered a big bungalow 14, Firoze Shah Road from Rajya Sabha pool and allotted it to AIMC. The place was in prime area of New Delhi, very close to Parliament and other important government establishments and agencies.

ZR constituted the new working committee with himself as President, and Kasim Ali Abid as the only General Secretary; since he wanted that no other person should be bracketed with him as General Secretary. I felt humiliated as there was world of difference between me and the new face of the Momin Conference, Kasim Ali Abid as he could not have measured upto my standing and experience in the organization. Moreover, he was till then a little known figure for the Momin community. For the first time, I saw him in Delhi when he was a regular visitor to meet late A.Q. Ansari in his western court official suit while he was in Rajya Sabha. Kasim Ali Abid was a serious contender for a Rajya Sabha ticket from Andhra Pradesh. Having no other choice, ZR nominated me as Secretary of AIMC and Secretary Incharge of central office at Delhi. Abdul Hai Ansari of Delhi, a dedicated person of the Momin Conference, as the treasurer. Senior most Momin-Congress leader from Bengal, Abdur Rauf Ansari, Swaleh Ansari of Varanasi who later became the mayor of Varanasi, Ashfaque Vaziri of Bhadohi, Amin Ansari of Mau Aema and Haroon Ansari from Malgaon, Maharashtra, were nominated as vice-presidents. Bihar had a good share in the working committee with Maulvi Saminuddin, M.P and Maulvi Sami Nadvi as its members. Maulvi Habibur Rahman Nomani an important Momin activist from U.P. was made president of U.P. unit. Karnataka was represented by Tajuddin Nawaz Bhai.

The leadership of the Momin movement was now in relatively younger hands. He picked up the thread where A.Q. Ansari had left. Momin community, all over the country, had great hopes in his young leadership. Through Momin Conference, Z.R. Ansari had greater plans and sincerely wanted educational upliftment and economic emancipation of the downtrodden Momin-Ansari community. ZR was a great orator. He imitated Maulana Azad, his political icon.

Given the responsibility, I settled down to my work of organising the central office of the All India Momin Conference at 14, Firozeshah Road in Delhi. It was the main thoroughfare for commuters to the central secretariat, different ministries like Railways, Agriculture, Defence, Home and External Affairs besides the Parliament House. Our central office with a huge hoarding, worked as self publicity for the organization. As a result, within a short period, Momin Conference was a much known organization for the Delhites. Since the central office had a very big and comfortable accommodation, Momin leaders from all over the country mostly Bihar, U.P. and Bengal, used to stay in the office during their visit to the national capital. It was a great facility for those associated with Momin Conference. Even Congress Muslim leaders and activists, other than of the community coming to meet central leaders also enjoyed courtesy of the Momin Conference in Delhi. The present NCP leader Tarique Anwer, was the blue eyed boy of Congress treasurer, Sitaram Kesri, incidentally both from Bihar. Being a seasoned politician, Kesri enjoyed confidence of the Congress High Command. He had the nack to pick up young and promising boys from his state to groom them as political activists, first through NSUI, the student wing of the Congress and then through youth Congress. Tarique headed this group of youngsters. Kesri was sincere towards that end since he even spent his personal money on their journeys to Delhi and back too, frequently. One has yet to find such a dedicated leader of the party in Congress. Tarique Anwer was at that time making frequent trips to Delhi with his group of young supporters being a serious contender for the presidentship of Bihar Youth Congress. He along with his troop stayed twice in my central office. Later in their lives, most of them became ministers and M.Ps. But they all remembered those days when they stayed with me in the central office of the All India Momin Conference. With my presence there, a large number of prominent persons from different shades of life used to come in the office which made it a hub of socio-political activities. Among frequent visitors, as I remember a few names now, were Bihar Minister Syed Ali Warsi; Dy. Speaker, West Bengal assembly, Kalimuddin Shams; prominent Urdu journalist Jamuna Das Akhtar; Journalist and Member of Parliament Hayatullah Ansari; my friends from Patna, Haroon Rashid, who later became Chairman of Bihar Minority Commission; Syed Razi Haider, Editor, *Sada-e-Aam*; besides large number of Congress-Momin leaders from all over the country. The central office of the All India Momin Conference remained always humming with life.

For the first time in its long history, All India Momin Conference had a full fledged central office in Delhi. Momin leaders from those states who till now, found themselves alienated from the activities of the organization had an opportunity to be in the midst of all activities.

In Delhi I could be able to get the help of Abdul Hai Ansari in day to day functioning of the office. He was originally from Amroha, U.P., settled in Delhi, engaged in painting contracts of banks and other central establishments. Even though he was a busy man in his profession, he would spare sufficient time to be with me in the central office. His presence in the office was of immense help to me. We had drafted yet another gentleman from Calcutta, Raziur Rahman Ansari of Narkuldanga. He was the most competent person to oversee our accounts section. In the course of time when the work load of the central office considerably increased and more so during the national session of the Momin Conference, he was entrusted with the task of internal audit, which he accomplished in a most satisfactory manner. Besides these two persons related to Momin movement, there were two more other persons in my team at the central office, one typist and another an assistant. With this small team, I was conducting the affairs of the central office of the All India Momin Conference in a most organised manner and to the full satisfaction of everybody related with the organization. In a very short period of its existence, it became a centre full of activities.

With all facilities at my command, I could make separate files for all the states, from Kashmir to Karnataka and Andhra Pradesh. For the first time in its history, it could be possible for the central office to have a list of office-bearers, members of the Working Committee and exhaustive list of prominent Momin leaders and activists of each and every state. This arrangement was quite handy for immediate contacts with related persons if and when such situation arose.

Ziaur Rahman Ansari took keen interest in the activities as the head of the organization. In Delhi, he would often drop and spend sometime with us, and whenever got an opportunity from his busy engagements of his ministry, he visited different places in order to keep personal contacts with the Momin leaders in the states. This resulted in better coordination and smooth working. After Z.R. Ansari took over, we both made extensive tours of West

Bengal, Bihar, U.P., Maharashtra and pre-dominant Momin areas of Old Delhi.

The president would occasionally invite media men, sometimes, exclusively Urdu press, Muslim members of Parliament, Congress president and other prominent central Congress leaders to the central office at lunch or dinner. We took the opportunity to host members of the All India Urdu Editor's Conference at dinner during its meeting at Delhi. Urdu editors from the entire country attended the dinner. Dr. Shankar Dayal Sharma, then a Union minister who later became the President of Indian Republic was delighted to visit our central office. In a considerably short period of its establishment, we could be able to have close liaison with every section of the people in Delhi.

The then Prime Minister Smt. Indira Gandhi and Congress President, D.K. Barooah showed keen interest in the activities of this historic organization. For his dynamism, suave manners, being highly cultured and dedicated to his responsibilities, Z.R. Ansari was the most favourite person in the Congress organization. He was a staunch Congress man and a strong pillar of secularism.

10th Session of All India Momin Conference, Delhi, 1976

In post independence period spanning about thirty years, the Momin Conference had two annual sessions, one in 1948 and the second was now being held at Delhi. Though, this was a long gap but the enthusiasm of the Momin-Ansar community towards their organization had not dwindled. It was in itself very encouraging. After fully satisfied with the spade work for more than six months which we jointly undertook, the Working Committee unanimously decided to hold the national session of the All India Momin Conference at Delhi. Delhi had hosted 6th session in 1943 and the last session the 9th in the series, was held at Patna in the year 1948.

The political situation of Delhi was tense in the year 1976 during the emergency. The infamous Turkman gate episode known for compulsory vasectomy of Muslims, when bulldozers of the Delhi administration mercilessly bull dozed houses of poor Muslims claiming innocent lives, had caused anger and resentment amongst Muslims all over the country. In Delhi political circles, there was a hush hush silence and no Muslim leader or organization dared to speak against government's undemocratic act that smelt communal bias. As is well known, Sanjay Gandhi who was commanding extra constitutional power during emergency was instrumental behind this carnage.

When some members suggested May, 1976 to hold the 10th session in Delhi, it was opposed by others of the Working Committee on the plea that since the atmosphere was charged with emotions, it was not wise to hold the session that might cause embarrassment to their leader, Z.R. Ansari. They were also of the opinion that participants from outside Delhi might hesitate to attend the session and thus, it may result in a flop. Z.R. Ansari was quick to overrule all objections and expressed his firm resolve to hold the session right in the back drop of the Turkman gate episode. He reminded the members that the Momin Conference always stood firmly against all sorts of injustices and communal bias without any fear in the past, therefore, we should not shy away from our responsibilities and better live upto its traditions. Expressing his strong determination, Ansari stunned the members that he would like none other than the Prime Minister Indira Gandhi to inaugurate the session. Under such odd circumstances, a bold expression from the president, the Working Committee unanimously approved his suggestion.

Since the Working Committee had already taken the decision, it was an uphill task to hold the session in Delhi with all apprehensions about its success. Besides that, finance was also a difficult problem before the leadership.

One late evening, the president rang me to meet him immediately to discuss something very important. When I met him accordingly, he conveyed me that he had received a call from Congress President D.K. Barooah to see him to discuss something about the proposed session. President wanted me to accompany him and keep secret about all this.

Next morning, as scheduled, we both went to D.K. Barooah's residence. I had little acquaintance with him while he was the Governor of Bihar before shifting to Delhi for his new assignment. I often used to meet him as a Congress man and journalist. His memory was too sharp as when Z.R. Ansari introduced me he said that he knew me from the period while he was at Patna. He made detailed enquiry about the session from Z.R. Ansari. After hearing the details he asked about the expenditure and opened up that Indiraji had asked him to find out the financial involvement in the session so that Congress could help. Without any pause or hesitation Z.R. Ansari told him plainly that he would not like to accept any financial help from the party as the community itself can fully contribute to make the Delhi session a grand success. Barooah was taken aback on Ansari's refusal and wondered how the community alone could take the entire burden on itself.

Z.R. Ansari was quite friendly to everybody and nice at heart but was strong in principles. He, as president of the self respecting community never appreciated any sort of financial help from outside the community least the Congress party. Coming back to his residence he was fuming over the suggestion made by Congress president. He called a special meeting of the Working Committee to discuss the financial requirements for the proposed session and to chalk out programmes for arranging the funds well before the work starts.

There was mixed reaction when the president gave details of our meeting and the offer made by the Congress president. However, majority of the members fully endorsed Ansari's firm stand against the offer and resolved that we on our own will raise funds to meet the entire expenditure.

This came as blessing in disguise. The entire leadership took it as a challenge. To begin with, I was told to visit Bengal first to meet Momin leaders and prominent individuals of the community from Bihar whom I personally knew since long.

At Calcutta alongwith the prominent Bengal Momin leader Abdur Rauf Ansari, I met Farzand Ali of Yatimmia & Sons, Abdul Qaiyum, Proprietor of Aminia Hotel, Haji Shamshuddin, Calcutta Paints in Dhramtallah Street and Master Qasim, a pioneer in Hawai Chappals at Topsia. My visit to these gentlemen was quite fruitful. They all responded generously except Haji Shamshuddin who had a desire to meet Z.R. Ansari whom he could not yet meet. Next week, we both flew to the Bengal capital. Haji Shamshuddin was overwhelmed by such a quick response from the president which he least expected. While at Calcutta, Z.R. Ansari took the opportunity to meet all those who had generously contributed towards holding the proposed national conference at Delhi. His Calcutta visit and meeting with the Momin community there had a sobering effect on the community.

In Bihar, Member of Parliament, Maulvi Saminuddin was the most sincere person towards providing his share of contribution for holding national meet at Delhi. He had been a grass-root politician. He travelled across his constituency, appealed to members of the Momin community to contribute generously towards this end. He made one person incharge, each for a cluster of villages. Maulvi Saminuddin invited us at his village home. He took us in his open jeep through the route that covered entire area of his constituency. On the way, welcome gates were erected where group of Momin workers welcomed the president and handed over to him purse of their most valued contribution. One thing that was clearly noticeable was that there was great enthusiasm amongst the Momin community, wherever we went. That was more encouraging for us more than the contribution we received. Another person, Dr. Mahmood Alam, eminent surgeon of Jamshedpur also made handsome contribution for the session. Dr. Alam is the eldest son of Md. Yahya, former Member of Bihar Public Service Commission and one of the founding fathers of this organization at Calcutta. Dr. Md. Matiullah and Md. Salim Ansari, Yarn Merchant of Gaya also made valuable contribution to make the session a great success. Salim Ansari attended the Delhi session with his wife and children.

In Uttar Pradesh, Swaleh Ansari of Benares, Ashfaque Vaziri and Naimullah Ansari of Bhadohi and a large number of Momin leaders and workers of the state arranged handsome contributions to make the national meet at Delhi a success. Maulvi Md. Vakil, Sitapur; Abdus Sattar, M.L.A., Bijnor; Babu Ashfaque, Moradabad; Khurshid Ahmad, Amroha; and many others enthusiastically contributed to the success of the Delhi session. Delhi had been a strong centre of the movement since its early days. Most of the old Delhi areas including Lal Darwaza, Ballimaran, Gali Qasim Jaan, Lal Kuan, Bara Hindu Rau, and Urdu Bazar etc. have large number of Momin Ansar habitants. Across Jamuna, Khuraiji with a strong Momin population, is famous for powerloom industry.

With the conference scheduled in Delhi, the Momin community everywhere was in upbeat mood. It was being held after a long time, the last being in Patna in the year 1948.

Gandhi Darshan at the bank of river Yamuna along the Ring Road where Indira Gandhi Indoor Stadium was later built during Asiad Games, originally, was a barren sandy land. About a year earlier, the Jamaet-e-Islami Hind held national meet of its organization. When we applied for the traditional Ram Lila ground, it was rejected on security grounds as it was nearer to the Turkman Gate. Instead, the same Gandhi Darshan was allotted to Momin Conference also. Since there was no structure on the land, every arrangement from a huge pandal, seating arrangement for one lakh persons under Shamiana, make shift bath rooms, toilets, tents in thousands were needed to be erected for the purpose. It was a gigantic task, indeed.

Months in advance, dates for the national meet were announced. All care was taken to see that the information reached to the community in every nook and corner. News items were published in prominent Urdu newspapers in states. Within days of the publication of the news, the central office started receiving letters enquiring details. The response was amazing for us. Sensing tremendous response and enthusiasm of the people, we requested in writing to the railway ministry for issuing sanction of 'single fare return journey' concession for the delegates attending the national meet as per rule. Minister of state for railways Shafi Qureshi was helpful to us in this regard. Once I got the orders and a copy of duly numbered and signed form, got its copies in thousands and sent the forms to different states, Momin members of Parliament and state legislatures, prominent Momin leaders and others. For Momin-Ansaris, once again it was a festive occasion. In fact, the entire Muslim community was watching with deep interest the ongoing preparations full of enthusiasm with a definite feeling of relief after a long hush-hush atmosphere preceeding the Turnkaman Gate excesses. It was indeed a welcome change. The venue of the 10th annual session was named "Abdul Qaiyum Ansari Nagar" while a number of gates erected at the venue were named after distinguished leaders of the movement since its inception. A huge pandal was set up to accommodate VIP guests and top leaders of the Momin Conference. The backdrop of the pandal was adorned with a huge flag of the organisation.

It was with a team work that the entire area looked like a small township. Massive arrangements were made from drinking water to wash rooms considering the presence of expectedly large number of delegates. Few tea stalls with eateries and book stalls were also set up. A beautiful park with flower plants were laid down at the entrance of the venue.

For the scheduled two-day session, arrangements were made

by the organizing committee for free lunch and dinner for the delegates coming from outside. The convener of the food sub-committee was entrusted with the responsibility of arranging a huge temporary kitchen. Buses were hired to carry the delegates from Delhi and New Delhi stations to the venue of the session. A team of volunteers drawn mostly from western part of U.P., Amroha, Meerut, Moradabad besides those from Delhi itself, were trained in advance to bring delegates from stations and inter state bus depot. The reception committee with its chairman Hafiz Abdul Aziz was in full command of the massive preparations. The Souvenir sub-committee had entrusted the responsibility of printing a most informative and a beautiful souvenir to Md. Yaqub Ansari of Old Delhi. A very prominent Urdu journalist of Delhi, Salamat Ali Mehdi was specially requisitioned to interview the president. That turned out to be a priced contribution to the magazine. Delegates from Assam, Orissa, Bengal, Bihar, U.P., Maharashtra, M.P., Punjab, Haryana started pouring since morning a day before the scheduled two-day session. It was one of the largest congregation of Muslims in Delhi after independence. By evening and since early morning on the day of the session, stream of delegates from far and near made a bee line to the venue. It presented a scene as if all roads lead to the Gandhi Darshan venue of the session. The significant aspect was the thrill and exitement of the community to attend the national meet. This was indeed a very encouraging sign for the leaders of the community as the adverse political atmosphere and the long gap after the last Patna session and the present one could not dampen the spirit of the people all over. The interest of the people could be judged from the fact that even from far away places like Bihar, people attended the session with their families.

The historic Delhi session started amidst all fanfare.The infamous Turkman gate episode was so fresh in the minds that the media was expecting some fireworks in the speeches of the top leaders.

Smt. Indira Gandhi was profusely garlanded and welcomed warmly by the President and other top Momin-Congress leaders on her arrival. The mammoth crowd gave a big ovation to Smt. Gandhi. She was visibly moved by the tremendous reception at the Momin meet, which she might not have been expecting in context of what had happened at Turkman gate recently. Chairman of the Reception Committee Hafiz Abdul Aziz read out the welcome address. In his speech, President of the All India Momin Conference and Union Minister Z.R. Ansari gave a short history of the Momin Conference, its glorious role in the freedom struggle and its strong opposition to the demand of a separate State for Indian muslims. He remembered those who founded the organization initially to fight out the evils that had plagued the Muslim society of the Indian sub-continent since centuries. The audience had a pleasant surprise when Z.R. Ansari, pointing his fingers towards the crowd, expressed his delight that two of the founder members from Calcutta were also attending the session. There was a bit of commotion in the crowd as every body wanted to have a glimpse of these senior leaders. He paid rich tributes to the last president and icon of the Momin movement, Abdul Qaiyum Ansari. The president while referring to the Turkman Gate brutalities, grim in face and harsh in his words, condemned the excesses on the poor Muslims by the Delhi administration in unequivocal terms. Ansari was given repeated applause by the crowd for his bold views and the way he had chosen to unfold the wounded sentiments of the Muslims as a whole on the face of the Prime Minister herself. She had the taste of the anger of the Muslim leadership even within the Congress over the excesses under the emergency rule. The Prime Minister listened every word aptly for criticising her government by none else other than her senior colleague itself.

Indira Gandhi was a shrewd politician. She kept cool and wisely chose not to react. When she first arrived at the venue, she got a tumultuous welcome from the crowd. Her memory about the patriotic role of the Momin Conference during freedom movement and the tremendous and unparallel support the entire Momin community gave to the Congress party, was refreshed when she listened every word from Z.R. Ansari. She as the leader of the nation, never wanted to loose the support of the community. She struck the right cord and at the very outset of her speech, expressed her delight to see the founder members of the organization present in the conference. On her request, both Maulana Md. Yahya and Abu Shams Abdul Ghaffoor from Calcutta, were escorted to the dias by the volunteers and made them sit there. This gesture by the Prime Minister was responded by thunderous applause and, once again, the atmosphere had changed. Indira Gandhi showered praises on the Momin community for its patriotic role during the freedom movement and said that the Momins scripted history that cannot be erased from the pages of the Indian history. Paying tributes to late Abdul Qaiyum Ansari she said that Ansari Saheb was not only the leader of the Momin community alone, he was the great strength for the Congress party as well.

Coming down to the vasectomy programme, she said that the nation must fight out the menace of fast growing population that had retarded growth. It was a national problem and everyone had the responsibility to lend its support to the movement. Indira Gandhi strongly supported the vasectomy programme of the government, decried the controversy and said that religion should not come in its way. The inaugural session ended on a cheerful note. There was sense of satisfaction on both sides. Momin leadership was happy that it could convey the feelings of the entire Muslim community in strongest words on the face of the highest government functionary. The Prime Minister was equally satisfied with the repeated applause from the mammoth crowd despite her firm stand on the policy of family planning. Before leaving, Indira Gandhi, on her desire, posed a photograph with both the founder leaders of the Momin movement. She was given a hearty send off.

As the history turned its pages, after the assassination of the Prime Minister, Indira Gandhi, her son Rajiv Gandhi was elected the next Prime Minister of the country. Though novice to active parliamentary politics, in a very short period, he started showing his mettle. Rajiv Gandhi proved himself a visionary and statesman. He wanted to take India to great heights, a place of high dignity in the entire world. He inherited the legacy of secular thinking and broad mindedness of his grand father, Nehru and mother, Indira. Throughout his career as the Prime Minister of the country, on several occasions, he was under pressure from the communal elements but he refused to act in that direction. The worst came during the controversial judgement of the Chief Justice of India on Shah Bano case. Indian Muslims felt betrayed and the community was restless over interference in their personal law guaranteed under Constitution. The media and the BJP blew the Shah Bano case to high proportions. A strong wind of communal passion griped the country.

The controversial judgement of Chief Justice Chandra Chud came for discussion in parliament. Union Minister Ziaur Rahman Ansari, both religious and nationalist, during his hours of two-day historic speech in Parliament, declared that the Constitution of India was supreme that gave guarantee to the minorities of the Secular Democratic India to safeguard their religious interests and the Supreme Court had no right to interfere with the Constitution. For his unmatched oratory skill and out of strong conviction, Ansari left no room for dissent. Prime Minmister Rajiv Gandhi was fully convinced and for that every sensible Indian agreed with Ansari's views.

Ansari had to pay a heavy price for his bold and unshakable stand. First, it was the Turkman Gate excesses that was so strongly condemned by him and now, his firm stand against the decision of Supreme Court in Shah Bano case did not go well with the communal elements. The communal fascist elements ganged up with like minded elements even within the U.P. Congress, who were known traditionally against the dynamic figure from the Momin-Ansar community and hatched a conspiracy to tarnish the public image of Z.R. Ansari. Ansari gave blood to the party and, on the basis of his selfless service only, made a tremendous rise in popularity to reach the highest position in the government. This made him the cynosure of their eyes.

Ansari was shocked beyond imagination since his firm stand to save the secular image of the government and for that, the nation, was not appreciated rather disliked by the diehard communal class of politicians, and also few government functionaries and the media. He was shocked because he, his family and the entire Momin community created history during freedom movement in opposing communal politics of the Muslim League. A great service to the nation, indeed.

Falling health coupled with deep frustration in public life completely broke him. Subsequently, there was a major political change at the centre. Congress was dethroned and the United Opposition came to power. The Muslim face in the BJP, Sikander Bakht, became the Urban Development Minister. Momin Conference, because of its secular credentials and strong anti-communal ideology, the opposition, more so, the BJP always considered it to be an ally of the Congress party. After assuming office, the first thing Bakht did that he got issued an urgent notice to vacate our office at 14, Ferozeshah Road and even threatened to take legal action against us if not vacated within the specified period. This was a vindictive step of BJP. However, in the meantime another bungalow at a stone throw distance on the same road was allotted to Member Rajya Sabha, Kasim Ali Abid, the general secretary. He agreed to lend us a portion of it, where we shifted. It could not accommodate the entire office. It all caused great setback. All these adverse developments caused a damping affect on the spirit of the community everywhere. Its leader was ailing and so, in real sense, the entire community seemed to be ailing. The way Z.R. Ansari was humiliated for his firm stand to refuse to compromise on the secular principles of the party and its government on the two major issues affecting Muslims, the second major community, was a pointer to the political atmosphere in the country. He faced the onslaught of the BJP and other like minded communal elements in the absence of strong support from the party and its leadership. It was the beginning of the dilution of the secular ideology of the Congress party, in a big way.

Ansari wanted that now somebody else should be elected to shoulder the responsibility of the Momin Conference. In fact, the organization lacked a strong and able leader like Abdul Qaiyum Ansari and Z.R. Ansari, who gave dynamic and sagacious leadership to the organization in post-independent India. Both these leaders had clean and unblemished political career.

In U.P., Maulana Habibur Rahman Nomani was a senior Momin leader. He was M.L.C and Chairman of the Etawah Sugar Mill. Later, he was nominated to Rajya Sabha. He unsuccessfully contested leadership election at Patna but could not get favour from even a single member of the Working Committee. Since then, he led a small group of frustrated Momin activists in U.P. against Z.R. Ansari. One of his closest aide was Md. Amin Ansari from Mau-Aema, Allahabad who later deserted him and joined the mainstream. He was also nominated to the Rajya Sabha. He went on Haj pilgrimage and died there.

Another small group from Bihar, though not openly against the leadership, found the situation favourable to get Nomani to the highest post. They claim that they were able to get Nomani's name cleared by Z.R. Ansari for the highest post but no Working Committee was called to formally elect a new leader. Neither Kasim Ali Abid, as general secretary nor myself as secretary, issued any letter to call WC meeting. The group declared Nomani as the next president. This was not accepted by the Working Committee and it declared that Ansari continued to be the president.

A victim of humiliation for no fault of his own, Z.R. Ansari could not bear the shock. He did not live long and died as a hero of the oppressed Muslim community of the country. At the fag end of his life and political career, he was the most frustrated person. His life and achievements will go down in the contemporary Indian history as the fighter against communalism and an unadulterated nationalist. He will be remembered as one of the greatest Indian of the post independence era who lived and died to uphold the secular credentials of the country.

In his death, the Muslim community of India lost a most courageous and trust worthy leader. After the death of Abdul Qaiyum Ansari, he gave a strong stewardship to the movement and maintained its high traditions.

Ansari did not survive long and succumbed to his ailment. The eventful era of Z.R. Ansari ended. Once again gloom overtook the entire community.

Abdur Rauf Ansari

Momin Conference lost its second president since 1947. Abdur Rauf Ansari, a senior Congress leader of Bengal, was a minister in state cabinet and vice-president of the party. A senior most Momin leader of the country and one of the vice-presidents of the Momin organization. He was the most deserving and suitable candidate for the top most post. He was elected the next president of the All India Momin Conference by the Working Committee. A.R. Ansari, was a good orator in Bengali and Urdu languages, a seasoned politician and a grass root Momin leader most successful within his state. He was a noble soul. His falling health could not make it possible for him to tour different parts of the country and make frequent visits to the national capital. He could not measure up to the capability of his last two predecessors which he honestly realized. He wanted to be relieved of this responsibility but there was acute dirth of any suitable leader at the top. Only within few years, A.R. Ansari died. Once again a void was created, difficult to be filled. Nomani as the leader of a handful of disgruntled Momin activists also could not make any stride. Those who were with him were upset with his style of working and partisan attitude in organizational matters. He also died in a very short period. Momin Conference lost its top leaders in quick succession.

The movement though initiated in 1913 but took formal shape in 1924 during the period when there was an upsurge against the British rule in the country. While the nation was exceptionally united under Indian National Congress, RSS and Hindu Maha Sabha was singing a different tune not congenial for the solidarity of the nation. On another side, Muslim League was harping on separate homeland for Muslims.

The Momin-Ansaris of India, who formed the majority group among Indian Muslims but the most downtrodden, came out to join the mainstream of freedom movement. The entire story of the movement is that of courage, conviction, determination and sacrifice. It is preserved in the pages of history and will be read in the country and abroad, even centuries after.

Shah Bano Case

The fascist elements in India led by RSS and its political wing, Jan Sangh (now BJP), have been consistently opposing Muslim Personal Law. They have been demanding scraping of separate personal law for the Muslims and imposition of Common Civil Code in its place. It is one of the cardinal items of their exhaustive list of agenda based on their basic policy of opposing everything that tends to provide separate identification to Indian Muslims. They want complete annihilation of Muslim identity and assimilation in Hindu culture and even religion, with the passage of time. It has been their sacred mission towards fulfillment of their resolve to establish a theocratic state in this country, at a time when a strong wind of democracy was blowing across the world. Even the only Hindu Kingdom on the globe vanished and now, Nepal has joined the long list of democratic countries.

Shah Bano case is a very interesting one. The saffron brigade with the open support of the print media (electronic media was not so developed then) held the nation to ransom over this case. Is it not strange that the same elements who religiously practice the ideology of communal hatred that led to the killings of women and children in brutal manners during anti-Muslim riots spread over last six decades, could suddenly develop soft heart for an old divorced Muslim woman over the issue of maintenance?

Shah Bano was an old lady of 70 years from the princely state of Indore. In her old age, she was divorced by her husband. Before coming to the main point, let me briefly put down that such cases have also been taken care of by the Islamic Shariat. However, RSS could find this as a most opportune case to attack Muslim Personal Law on humanitarian ground and demanded imposition of

Common Civil Code. They managed to file a case against the Shariat Law on her behalf by their men in the lower court and made an appeal with the court to scrap Shariat law in this case. The lower courts rejected the appeal that it deserved most. When the case came up for hearing in the Supreme Court, Justice Chandra Chud was the Chief Justice. He gave most controversial judgement that took the nation by surprise. Muslims, who respect and abide by the law of the land in all civil and criminal cases, have the constitutional guarantee to practice their own religion and follow the Shariat Law. The court has no authority to subvert this and take away the constitutional right granted to its citizens. Indian media baring the Muslim press, failed to support a very genuine demand of justice from the distressed Muslim community and display a high standard of unbiased journalism. Instead media put its entire weight behind the RSS-BJP-VHP onslaught on Indian Muslims and accused the community of being 'obscurantist'. The media projected Indian Muslims as separatists and branded Islam as a religion against the rights of its women. They carried a nasty propaganda against Islam and Muslims.

Once again, frustration overtook the entire Muslim community. Presentations of memorandum from Muslim organizations, their members in parliament and state legislatures, other political leaders, rallies and conferences against Chandra Chud's judgement could not bring any relief from the government. Muslims were upset over Chandra Chud's ruling since it was in total negation of the sprit of the Constitution and brazen interference in Muslim Shariat Law. The saffron brigade spearheaded a planned movement throughout the country in favour of Supreme Court judgement and created communal tension. In India, Muslims were at the receiving end. They have no political strength. The RSS (BJP) has found a good number of seats in both houses of Parliament that gave it the required political strength.

Rajiv Gandhi was the then Prime Minister of India. He was dynamic and, by and large, free from narrow communal outlook. His cabinet had a senior minister in Mr. Z.R. Ansari and Mr. Arif Mohammad Khan, a junior Muslim minister.

Mr. Ziaur Rahman Ansari who came from Unnao in U.P. had a rich nationalist background. His father was twice a Congress member of U.P. assembly. Both, father and son were deeply associated with the movement. Z.R. Ansari was a religious man.

He was also very much disturbed over Supreme Court order in Shah Bano case as any other Muslim of the country. The entire Muslim community was restless as the judgement was a brazen move from the highest seat of judiciary to interfere with the religious interest and constitutional right of Muslims.

His junior colleague in the cabinet, Arif Mohammad Khan was a new comer to the Congress party. He was the former president of Aligarh Muslim University Student Union. During discussions on Shah Bano Case Supreme Court judgement in Parliament, Arif Mohammad Khan chose to defend the judgement. His arguments in favour of Chadra Chud's judgement shocked the Muslim community as he tried to project himself as a 'progressive Muslim' and ruthlessly advocated against the Shariat law, perhaps against his own conscience to please his masters in the party and the government since till the other day, he was known for his strong pro-Muslim bias as the fire brand AMU agitationist. Muslims were shocked over his 'tailored' outburst against the Muslim Shariat. Z.R. Ansari was equally upset over Arif Mohammad Khan's attitude of apathy towards Muslims and Shariat law more so because he was the son-in-law of his close acquaintance, Editor of *Siyasat Jadid,* Kanpur, Ishaque Ilmi, known for his strong pro-Muslim views. Ansari believed that Muslim leaders in the government must stand against any injustice meted out to the community while representing the community in the party or the government, it was obligatory to defend and speak strongly against injustice without any fear.

Z.R. Ansari prepared himself well to present the case of the Indian Muslims strictly in the light of Shariat law in its right perspective. He burned the midnight oil to deeply study the Shariat law and the related Surah in the holy Quran in respect of the provision of maintenance of a divorced lady. Fully equipped with facts, Ansari met Rajiv Gandhi and expressed his desire to present before the law makers the lacunae in the judgement in the Shah Bano case. He told the Prime Minister that Muslims across the country were genuinely agitated as the highest court had ignored their constitutional right. He also made it clear that his arguments would go against the controversial judgement. Rajiv Gandhi was a reasonable and intelligent person. He could sense the distress of his cabinet minister over such a sensitive religious issue and gave him permission to speak in Parliament.

Words went round that Ansari was going to oppose the Supreme Court judgement in Parliament and subsequently, a tirade was let loose against Ansari by the entire non-Muslim media alongwith the saffron brigade. Unruffled, Ansari entered the House with a load of Holy Quran, copies of Hadith, books on Shariat Law, copy of Indian Constitution and other related quotations. He was assisted by the staff of Lok Sabha who piled up the load on the desk. Such keen interest was never seen in any of the debates earlier. The entire House was full to its seats. Visitor's gallery was full with foreign diplomats and other dignitaries. National and international media packed the press gallery.

Ansari made a landmark speech defending the Constitutional right of the Muslims. The Union Minister was in his oratory excellence Lok Sabha had ever heard in the recent past. He smashed Chandra Chud's every clause of the judgement, one by one. He told the House that under the Indian Constitution, while pronouncing judgement, Supreme Court should have been guided by the Constitution. Being representatives of the people in this august house, it is our sacred duty to see that the Constitution was not bye-passed or overlooked by the judiciary.

Ansari spoke on the issue first on November 22, 1985 and again on Friday December 20, 1985.

He made a tension free speech full of wit and humour. He would occasionally quote popular Urdu couplets to drive home his point. There was pin drop silence in the House as the members were listening to Ansari's arguments with deep interest and curiosity except few interruptions from such members who had no interest in the dry subject.

Making a dig over the comment of the learned Chief Justice that 'the law has to be interpreted by the court with the mandate of Quran', Z.R. Ansari said, 'And the interpretations he will give. Now all these Ulemas, Muftis and Mujtahids should close down their offices. Mr. Chandra Chud is here to interpret Quran as a grand Mufti as a good Mujtahid of the time. Who else can come forward to interpret Quran as a reformer? The wording, the time and the style of the judgement, all these show that.....some learned man has prepared a paper for a seminar'.

Ansari spoke in length about Shariats clear provisions for marriage and divorce in Islam. He stressed that '*Sura Talaq*' should be read in its totality and not a few 'Ayats' only. Paying of maintenance has been stressed in Islam but it does not mean that it should go on for life. It is clearly mentioned in Ayat 6 of '*Sura Talaq*' that the divorcee is entitled to maintenance during the period of '*Iddat*' only. Ansari presented the case in a marvellous manner that was convincing and of full satisfaction to the members except those who never believed in reasoning.

Keeping in his mind about the members of the BJP and those of its like who show little regard for other religions, the Union Minister said that scriptures of different religions should be studied with a sense of faith and not with a biased mind. This is what is called National Integration as visualized by Mahatma Gandhi, Pandit Nehru and Maulana Azad. Secularism is having regard for each and every religion and not negation of religion.

Z.R. Ansari's marathon forceful speech was convincing. He had raised valid points that was not easy to be turned down. His arguments were based entirely on constitutional guarantee. The unprecedented courage of the Union Minister to go against the Supreme Court verdict was out of his unflinching faith in the secular democratic polity of the country. By doing so, he saved the Union government from being caught on the wrong foot and the country from political turmoil.

Ansari brought great relief to the restless Muslim community. He turned the table and saved the community from any interference in their religious matter. Being an activist of the Momin movement during the freedom struggle and nationalist to the core, he had the courage to fight out a calculated misadventure against the Indian Muslims by the saffronites.

However, as was very much expected, this did not augur well with the communal elements and by a section of the media as well. While the Indian Muslim community heaved a sigh of relief, Ansari earned wrath of the press in lieu of his patriotic gesture. Even today, years after the decision of the Rajiv government to undo the judgement through an act of parliament, Congress party is accused of 'vote bank' politics, 'appeasement' etc. The communal elements of the country have lately coined these words to bully the weak secular Congress governments so that they could desist from doing any justice to the Muslim community. And it is simply a hard fact that on most of the occasions, Congress governments got bullied. One should note the fact that it has become a ritual for the BJP, well known for its anti-Muslim policies, helped by a section of the media as well, always over zealous, spear-headed tirade against Indian Muslims. Even a responsible head of a constitutional body could not keep secret of his bigoted mind and went out of the way to issue a press statement demanding Ansari's dismissal from the union ministry. It was amazing to find that none from the Congress party nor the government cared to question his credentials for issuing such derogatory statement against the Union minister. This soft attitude of the government towards the communal and fascist elements in the country, on such occasions, emboldened them which mainly contributed to worsening of the communal situation of the country. However, I, as one of the activist of the Momin conference, found it my responsibility to issue a strong worded statement against the said chairman and demanded his immediate removal. The statement was prominently carried by Delhi edition of the paper on front page.

●●●